Spontaneous Melodramas 2

24 more impromptu skits that bring Bible stories to life

Spontaneous Melodramas 2

24 more impromptu skits that bring Bible stories to life

Doug Fields
Laurie Polich
Duffy Robbins

Youth Specialties

ZondervanPublishingHouse
Grand Rapids, Michigan

A Division of HarperCollinsPublishers

Spontaneous Melodramas 2: 24 more impromptu skits that bring Bible stories to life

Copyright © 2001 by Youth Specialties

Youth Specialties Books, 300 S. Pierce St., El Cajon, CA 92020, are published by Zondervan Publishing House, 5300 Patterson Ave. S.E., Grand Rapids, MI 49530.

Library of Congress Cataloging-In-Publication Data

Fields, Doug, 1962-
      Spontaneous melodramas 2: 24 more impromptu skits that bring Bible stories to life /
   Doug Fields, Laurie Polich & Duffy Robbins.
         p. cm.
      Includes index.
      ISBN 0-310-23300-3
Drama in Christian education. 2. Christian education of teenagers. 3. Bible plays,
   American. 4. Christian drama, American. I. Title: Spontaneous melodramas two. II. Polich,
   Laurie. III. Robbins, Duffy. IV. Title.

BV1534.4 .F54 2001
268'.67—d21

00-043880

Edited by Casey Finley and Lorna McFarland Hartman
Design and illustrations by Patton Brothers Design

Printed in the United States of America

01 02 03 04 05 06/VG/ 10 9 8 7 6 5 4 3 2 1

Contents

How to use Spontaneous Melodramas 2

Trying to explain the concept of spontaneous melodramas is like trying to explain the concept of a car wash. It's as simple as it sounds, but if you've never seen one before, it may be tough to visualize. Imagine the person who has never seen a car wash: "I drive my car through a building and it comes out cleaner on the other end, huh?"

A spontaneous melodrama is almost that simple.

It's a short play in which the acting is unrehearsed. As the narrator reads through the script, the actors act out the narration. If there's an acting part, they act it. If there's a speaking part, they speak. It's not meant to be serious theater—it's light, fun, and not too polished.

Yet in their simplicity, spontaneous melodramas demonstrate a basic educational principle: Students learn and retain more when they are involved in the learning process.

For example, teach a lesson on the importance of service and students walk away with—at best—a mandate: "I guess I should be serving others." Take those same kids on a mission trip to build houses, and they walk away with a life-changing memory. You don't have to be in youth ministry long to know that a memory trumps a mandate every time.

A spontaneous melodrama is a teaching tool to help make Bible passages memorable for your students. Our belief is that if you can get your students laughing, moving around the room, and involved in the teaching, they're more likely to remember the lesson. It's a tool to make God's Word vivid.

The process is simple.

1. Find a melodrama that fits your intended lesson. If you're teaching a particular topic (i.e. temptation, the power of God, God's love, faith, etc), choose one that ties into the topic. Or use it as an intro when you're teaching one of the 24 passages these melodramas are based on.

2. Prior to the meeting, do a quick inventory: How many characters are needed for the melodrama? What props are required? Read through the **Leader Hints**.

3. During your meeting, call up the students you need to play each part. In most cases, they don't need prior notice or a rehearsal. Just call them up and pass out the props. It's showtime!

4. And don't worry too much about getting everything right. This is not Steven Spielberg—more like Abbott and Costello. You may have to coach your students a little at first, but once they have their first experience acting goofy in front of the group, the comfort level comes pretty fast (especially when they get their first laugh.) Soon you may have a fight trying to keep them off the stage.

Spontaneity makes great humor, so plan for it!

Now and then, every youth worker has the experience of picking up a resource, trying an idea, and then watching as it bombs. The kids didn't get it. Nobody thought it was funny. And the natural complaint is, "That idea didn't work!" It's important to remember that ideas don't work, youth workers work. The ideas are simply the tools we use to do our work.

Most of these melodramas require little planning beyond gathering a few props—if that. But you'll find that some simple preparations may make the melodrama work better. Here are some suggestions to consider.

1. Casting pearls before...uh, casting students...

Who should I cast in the swine part? One of the keys to making a melodrama work is giving some thought to who should play each part. For example, you don't want someone quiet and shy to play the part of Cruella De Vil in **101 Damnations** (Luke 4:40-41), because that part requires someone who's willing to ham it up. If you assign that part to Susie Silent, you'll think you're experiencing the 102nd damnation instead.

On the other hand, you don't want the same five extroverts in every melodrama. There are some parts that will allow your quieter kids to shine. Maybe Tim Timid shouldn't be Samson, but he has all the ability and charisma needed to play one of the toppled pillars.

Remember that some kids respond well to parts that put them in silly situations, while others don't. If you're not sure how a student might respond, there's no rule from the IMC (the International Melodrama Commission) that says you can't talk to the student in advance about the part. If the part makes them uncomfortable, plug them in somewhere else. If you don't have a student to play an especially corny role, recruit a leader to step up and take the part.

2. Read it right and write while you're reading.

Without question, most important part of a melodrama is narration. Telling the story well is the key. There is no better way to mess up the melodrama than to stumble over words, lose your place, or miss the subtlety of a play on words. It doesn't mean you need to call in James Earl Jones as a guest narrator—just take a little time to read through the script out loud several times before going live. Get used to the names of Bible characters. Get a feel for the flow of the drama. Note what the actors should be doing. By doing this, you'll be more relaxed and spontaneous when you're reading in front of the group.

Sometimes the funniest stuff in a spontaneous melodrama is the stuff that happens—well, spontaneously. If a performer misunderstands your narration and does something not in the script, ad-lib a line to work it into the story. Don't feel you have to read the script exactly as it's written. Tweak it. Cut out a part that won't work for your group. Add a reference to last week's lock-in, or mention a person in your group by name —whatever it takes to help draw in your students ("Not only did Job lose his family, his farm, and his health—he was also a fan of the Philadelphia Eagles.").

3. Actions speak louder than words, so speak the actions loudly.

As you read through these melodramas you'll see right away they are intensely visual. Spontaneous melodramas are not known for extensive dialogue. Each melodrama is peppered with action words that invite your students to *do* something. This is important for making it work.

While you're narrating the melodrama, the actors will take their cues from what you say and the way you say it. You may find it helpful to go through the melodrama in advance and mark the verbs (uh, the action words) so you'll know when to pause and give your students a nonverbal cue. ("Samson groaned [pause]…sighed [pause]…grimaced [pause]…staggered [pause]…and screamed in agony [pause]…as his chest heaved with rage [pause]…")

Occasionally you may need to repeat a word or phrase to let them know some action is expected. "His…chest…heaved…with…rage. I said *heaved with rage.*" You get the point.

4. Don't show up the main showdown.

Behind all the silliness and fun in this resource is a deeply serious vision: that your students might come to have a genuine encounter with Jesus Christ.

Isn't that a lot to ask of a melodrama? You bet! So we better not ask the melodrama to do what only God can do. We have a God who speaks through lilies, fig trees, dried bones, and Old Testament donkeys—and he can speak through melodramas too.

But this book is the means to an end. We're not just trying to be funny, have fun, or get kids to think we're cool (don't worry—t hey won't!). What we *are* trying to do is stimulate their interest in the Word of God and the Lord it testifies about. A melodrama is not a Bible study. It may be part of a Bible study, or it may simply be a fun skit to develop an appetite for Bible study. But it's probably not a good idea to finish **Gilligan's Zoo** and say, "Okay, kids, let's close in prayer. That's it for the night."

We don't want to get so carried away with the vehicle we forget our destination. Our job is to draw kids closer to Christ—and that's a destination we get to by God's intervention as we encounter his word. Our prayer is that these melodramas will add fuel and laughter for the journey.

Have fun and may God bless you in your work.

Doug, Laurie, & Duffy

The making of Adam and Eve, Genesis 2

The Sumptuous Spare Rib

Bible Text

4 This is the account of the heavens and the earth when they were created.

When the Lord God made the earth and the heavens— 5and no shrub of the field had yet appeared on the earth and no plant of the field had yet sprung up, for the Lord God had not sent rain on the earth and there was no man to work the ground, 6but streams came up from the earth and watered the whole surface of the ground— 7the Lord God formed the man from the dust of the ground and breathed into his nostrils the breath of life, and the man became a living being.

8Now the Lord God had planted a garden in the east, in Eden; and there he put the man he had formed. 9And the Lord God made all kinds of trees grow out of the ground—trees that were pleasing to the eye and good for food. In the middle of the garden were the tree of life and the tree of the knowledge of good and evil.

10A river watering the garden flowed from Eden; from there it was separated into four headwaters. 11The name of the first is the Pishon; it winds through the entire land of Havilah, where there is gold. 12(The gold of that land is good; aromatic resin and onyx are also there.) 13The name of the second river is the Gihon; it winds through the entire land of Cush. 14The name of the third river is the Tigris; it runs along the east side of Asshur. And the fourth river is the Euphrates.

15The Lord God took the man and put him in the Garden of Eden to work it and take care of it. 16And the Lord God commanded the man, "You are free to eat from any tree in the garden; 17but you must not eat from the tree of the knowledge of good and evil, for when you eat of it you will surely die."

18The Lord God said, "It is not good for the man to be alone. I will make a helper suitable for him."

19Now the Lord God had formed out of the ground all the beasts of the field and all the birds of the air. He brought them to the man to see what he would name them; and whatever the man called each living creature, that was its name. 20So the man gave names to all the livestock, the birds of the air and all the beasts of the field.

But for Adam no suitable helper was found. 21So the Lord God caused the man to fall into a deep sleep; and while he was sleeping, he took one of the man's ribs and closed up the place with flesh. 22Then the Lord God made a woman from the rib he had taken out of the man, and he brought her to the man.

23The man said,

"This is now bone of my bones
    and flesh of my flesh;
she shall be called 'woman,'
    for she was taken out of man."

Cast

* Stream (girl)
* 3 trees
* Tree of Life (girl)
* Tree of Knowledge of Good and Evil (guy)
* Adam
* Bird (girl)
* Hyena (guy or girl)
* Monkey (small guy)
* Eve

Props

* Spray bottle filled with water for stream
* Piece of fruit for tree of life

As the scene opens...

The two trees should be onstage seated, with Adam lying between them.

In the beginning God made the heavens and the earth, but there was no rain to water the ground. So a stream rose up and ran around spreading her water all over the ground. *[She enters from the audience with her water bottle, spraying into the air as she enters.]* As she watered, several trees sprang up and spread their branches, forming a beautiful garden. In the middle of the garden were two trees: the tree of life, which stood tall, its arms stretched to the sky, and the tree of knowledge of good and evil, which stood rubbing its hands together, letting out a loud sinister laugh. In between the two trees there was a formless man, who lay there like he was part of the ground.

Suddenly the breath of God blew across the stage so powerfully that both trees were knocked to the ground. At that, the man started shaking, stood up, and celebrated his new form by making muscleman poses. The trees got to their feet—uh, their roots—and oohed and aahed. Then the audience oohed and aahed. The man's name was Adam, and he began immediately searching around the trees for food because he was very hungry. The bad tree yelled "Over here!" and reached out one of its branches, knocking Adam to the ground. The good tree reached out its branches, helped Adam up, and gave him a piece of fruit. Adam ate; but he still craved more.

God saw Adam's craving, so he made some animals that came running onstage and stood at attention in front of Adam. Adam pointed at the first animal and said, "Bird." The bird immediately celebrated her name by chirping and flying offstage. Then Adam pointed at the second animal and said, "Hyena." The hyena began to chuckle. Then he began laughing uncontrollably, fell to the ground, and rolled offstage. Adam pointed to the third animal and said, "Monkey." The monkey jumped on Adam's back and began picking through Adam's hair, searching for fleas. Adam dropped the monkey to the ground and shooed him away. The monkey ran offstage making loud monkey noises. After he named all the animals, Adam was still lonely, so he lay on his back and cried.

God put Adam into a deep sleep, and while Adam snored, he removed one of Adam's spare ribs. Suddenly a beautiful woman appeared. When Adam woke up and saw her, he stood up and said loudly, "Whoa!" Then he said, "Man!" Then he said both words together in a very loud voice. Eve smiled, pointed to herself and said, "Woman." Adam pointed to himself and said, "Man." They held hands and gazed into each other's eyes. That day Adam's craving ended.

END

Gilligan's Ark

Bible text

[5]The Lord saw how great man's wickedness on the earth had become, and that every inclination of the thoughts of his heart was only evil all the time. [6]The Lord was grieved that he had made man on the earth, and his heart was filled with pain. [7]So the Lord said, "I will wipe mankind, whom I have created, from the face of the earth—men and animals, and creatures that move along the ground, and birds of the air—for I am grieved that I have made them." [8]But Noah found favor in the eyes of the Lord.

Cast

* The Skipper (Noah)
* Gilligan (Ham)
* Mary Ann (Noah's wife)
* Dove
* God
* Flood waters (audience doing the wave)
* Storm (audience making rain and thunder noises)
* Animals (assigned to audience members by last name; feel free to combine letter groups for smaller audiences)

A-D: Dogs	N-P: Birds
E-F: Flies (buzz)	Q-S: Pigs
G-J: Bears (growl and roar)	T-Z: Wolf
K-M: Cows	

Props

* Sailors' hats (for Skipper and Gilligan)
* Old tie-dyed shirt with peace symbol
* Sign with GOD written on it
* Theme music from "Gilligan's Island" (go to "My Wav Theme Song Collection" site at www.members.tripod.com/~clockj/webdoc3.htm to download)

Play the theme music from "Gilligan's Island." As the music fades, the narration begins....

God looked out at his creation; it was a long, serious gaze. His angry frown and furrowed brow showed how ticked he was about all the wickedness he saw. He said, "We're going to have to clean this mess up."

That's when God called Skipper and his family. Skipper and his family bowed down before God and said, "We're not worthy, we're not worthy." And God said, "Well, Skipper, because of your right-eousness, believe it or not, you actually *are* worthy!" That made Skipper's son Gilligan, and Skipper's wife, Mary Ann, very happy. They jumped up and down ecstatically and hugged Skipper. Skipper, quite embarrassed, took off his hat and hit his son Gilligan.

Much to their surprise God waved his hands and said, "Hush. There's a flood coming, and you've got to get your ship together." Skipper, Gilligan, and Mary Ann gave a big sailor salute and shouted back, "Aye, aye, sir. What's a ship?" But they starting carrying boards back and forth, pounding nails, and stepping back importantly to look at their work, and pretty soon the ship was done. They high-fived each other, except for Gilligan, who had hit his thumb with the hammer and was hopping around on one foot clutching his injured hand and making a lot of "Ow" noises.

Skipper and his family loaded the animals. Each animal made its own noise as the ark was loaded. First came the bears. Then, the birds. Then came the cows, and the wolves. Then came the flies. Then came the pigs. These were Gilligan's favorite. He actually went over and hugged a pig or two—they needed to, like, bond. Then came the dogs, who were so happy to be on board that one of them lifted up his—no, not what you thought!—face, and began licking Mary Ann's face. She laughed and said, "Down, boy, or we'll find out if it's *really* true that dogs can dog-paddle."

As soon as the last animal was loaded a great storm arose.

[Audience makes storm noises.] It started out quietly. Then it got louder. Then it got quiet again; then suddenly it was huge and there was a great wave *[audience wave participation]*! And flood waters began to rise. First with just small waves, and then with huge waves. The animals shrieked with fear. Gilligan yelled out above the roar, "Skipper, you know what animals do when they get scared, so we better do something fast!" So Skipper began patting different animals on the head, tickling them under their chin, and scratching the back of their neck. While he did this he reminded them, "Don't worry, it's only a three-hour tour."

But in fact, after 40 days and 40 nights they were still huddled together on the boat, rocking back and forth with the waves smacking against the sides. That's when Skipper sent out a dove that went around the room looking for a dry place to land. As the dove flew around the room, he kept saying '60s phrases like "Peace, man," "Far out," and "Make sun, not rain." The storm was still raging, though, and the waves were still rolling, and he couldn't find a place to land. So he came back to the front of the room. He was bummed. It was a bad trip.

Two more weeks went by, and by this time the ark was way ripe. Mary Ann held her nose and said, "Man, we need a can of ark freshener!" Gilligan made gagging noises and said, "Hey, Skipper, have you been eating the dog's food again?" And Skipper, hitting Gilligan with his hat, yelled back, "Come on guys, it's stink or sink. We'll make it."

And sure enough, two weeks later, the dove went out around the room again, doing his '60s thing, making the peace sign with his wing, and saying, "It's Woodstock all over again, dudes. We're going back to the garden." And this time he didn't come back. He circled the room twice and was gone. The storm grew quieter and the waves began to die down. That's when Skipper yelled out, "LAND HO!" and pointed excitedly to dry land.

Gilligan and Mary Ann shouted, "Ahoy, matey," "Full steam

ahead," "Avast ye landlubbers," and "All paws on deck." The animals began to make noises of joy. Skipper, Gilligan, and Mary Ann looked up into the heavens and raised their hands in thanksgiving.

Despite the raging storm and flood, the three wayward sailors realized that God was always looking out for them.

[Play Gilligan's Island theme and fade out.]

END

Touched by an Angel

Bible Text

²²That night Jacob got up and took his two wives, his two maidservants and his eleven sons and crossed the ford of the Jabbok. ²³After he had sent them across the stream, he sent over all his possessions. ²⁴So Jacob was left alone, and a man wrestled with him till daybreak. ²⁵When the man saw that he could not overpower him, he touched the socket of Jacob's hip so that his hip was wrenched as he wrestled with the man. ²⁶Then the man said, "Let me go, for it is daybreak."

But Jacob replied, "I will not let you go unless you bless me."

²⁷The man asked him, "What is your name?"

"Jacob," he answered.

²⁸Then the man said, "Your name will no longer be Jacob, but Israel, because you have struggled with God and with men and have overcome."

²⁹Jacob said, "Please tell me your name."

But he replied, "Why do you ask my name?" Then he blessed him there.

³⁰So Jacob called the place Peniel, saying, "It is because I saw God face to face, and yet my life was spared."

Cast

* Jake the Snake
* Ee-so Hairy
* Rebekah
* Laban
* Rachel the Babe
* Leah the Blind
* Angel (a big guy)

Props

* Birthright (sheet of paper for Ee-so)
* Pillows (for Rachel and Leah)
* Ropes to create a boxing ring (optional)

Ee-so should be the guy in your group with the longest hair. When Rachel and Leah make their second entrance, they need to have pillows under their clothes to make it look like they are pregnant.

As the scene begins...

Jake the Snake strides out and begins striking poses.

Once upon a time there lived a great wrestler by the name of Jake the Snake. Every time Jake won a wrestling match, he would flex his muscles and yell loudly, "I'm the king of the world!" His mother Rebekah would stand behind him proudly applauding and admiring his muscles.

Jake had a twin brother named Ee-so Hairy, who challenged Jake to a wrestling match one day. Ee-so stepped up to the ring, fanning himself with his birthright, and stood in front of Jake flexing his big hairy muscles and combing his fingers through his hair. But Jake came from behind and grabbed Ee-so and pinned him to the ground. Ee-so accidentally let go of his birthright, and Jake snatched it, while Rebekah clapped wildly. Ee-so stormed offstage, flipping his hair and vowing to seek revenge.

Next Laban came out with his two daughters, Rachel the Babe and Leah the Blind, at his side. He pushed the girls out in front of him as bait to distract Jake. Jake took one look at Rachel and got weak in the knees, causing him to fall to the ground. Laban came over to pin Jake, but Jake miraculously regained his strength, and the fight began.

First Jake was on top of Laban, then Laban was on top of Jake. Finally, after what seemed like 14 years, Jake pinned Laban and won the fight. When he got up, Laban sulked his way offstage and Jake put one arm around Rachel and one arm around Leah, and sang, "We are family, I got both the sisters with me!" Rachel and Leah started to kiss Jake on the cheek, but Leah missed and kissed his nose instead. The two women said goodbye to their new husband and went offstage to arrange their home.

Jake was tired from the fight, so he stretched and lay down to sleep. Suddenly an angel appeared and stood over him. Trembling with fear, Jake got up and faced the angel. Eventually he grabbed the angel and wrestled him to the ground. (This boy is in bad need of a people skills seminar.) The angel reached out one finger and barely touched Jake on the hip, causing Jake to roll around the floor screaming in pain. Sure he had won the fight, the angel got up and started to walk away. Suddenly Jake grabbed his foot and said faintly, "I won't let you go." But a sudden sneeze forced him to let go of the angel's foot. The angel turned and said, "Bless you," and flew offstage.

In the instant Jake stood up he realized he was a new man. He had a new limp in his step and a new gentle spirit. He cried out to the audience, "I'm a lover, not a fighter." Rachel and Leah came out onstage on either side of Jake and pointed to their pregnant stomachs, proving his statement was true. And that was how Israel began.

END

Joseph and Potiphar's wife, Genesis 39

The Proposition

Bible text

¹ Now Joseph had been taken down to Egypt. Potiphar, an Egyptian who was one of Pharaoh's officials, the captain of the guard, bought him from the Ishmaelites who had taken him there.

²The Lord was with Joseph and he prospered, and he lived in the house of his Egyptian master. ³ When his master saw that the Lord was with him and that the Lord gave him success in everything he did, ⁴ Joseph found favor in his eyes and became his attendant. Potiphar put him in charge of his household, and he entrusted to his care everything he owned. ⁵ From the time he put him in charge of his household and of all that he owned, the Lord blessed the household of the Egyptian because of Joseph. The blessing of the Lord was on everything Potiphar had, both in the house and in the field. ⁶ So he left in Joseph's care everything he had; with Joseph in charge, he did not concern himself with anything except the food he ate.

Now Joseph was well-built and handsome, ⁷ and after a while his master's wife took notice of Joseph and said, "Come to bed with me!"

⁸ But he refused. "With me in charge," he told her, "my master does not concern himself with anything in the house; everything he owns he has entrusted to my care. ⁹ No one is greater in this house than I am. My master has withheld nothing from me except you, because you are his wife. How then could I do such a wicked thing and sin against God?" ¹⁰ And though she spoke to Joseph day after day, he refused to go to bed with her or even be with her.

¹¹ One day he went into the house to attend to his duties, and none of the household servants was inside. ¹² She caught him by his cloak and said, "Come to bed with me!" But he left his cloak in her hand and ran out of the house.

¹³ When she saw that he had left his cloak in her hand and had run out of the house, ¹⁴ she called her household servants. "Look," she said to them, "this Hebrew has been brought to us to make sport of us! He came in here to sleep with me, but I screamed. ¹⁵ When he heard me scream for help, he left his cloak beside me and ran out of the house." ¹⁶ She kept his cloak beside her until his master came home.

¹⁷ Then she told him this story: "That Hebrew slave you brought us came to me to make sport of me. ¹⁸ But as soon as I screamed for help, he left his cloak beside me and ran out of the house."

¹⁹ When his master heard the story his wife told him, saying, "This is how your slave treated me," he burned with anger. ²⁰ Joseph's master took him and put him in prison, the place where the king's prisoners were confined.

But while Joseph was there in the prison, ²¹ the Lord was with him; he showed him kindness and granted him favor in the eyes of the prison warden. ²² So the warden put Joseph in charge of all those held in the prison, and he was made responsible for all that was done there. ²³ The warden paid no attention to anything under Joseph's care, because the Lord was with Joseph and gave him success in whatever he did.

23

Cast

* Joseph
* Potiphar
* Potiphar's wife
* Tree (one guy)
* Table (two guys)
* Crowd (the audience)

Props

* Ax (rolled-up newspaper)
* Broom
* Rug

Leader hints

Instruct the audience to cheer wildly each time you say THE LORD WAS WITH JOSEPH.

As the scene begins...

Joseph is onstage sweeping.

An Egyptian official named Potiphar had purchased Joseph, a Hebrew slave. THE LORD WAS WITH JOSEPH as he lived in the household of his Egyptian master. One day while Joseph was sweeping around the house Potiphar came in to see how he was doing. He watched Joseph pick up the rugs from the floor and beat them till they were clean. He saw Joseph chopping firewood with an axe. Potiphar noticed that THE LORD WAS WITH JOSEPH, and he put him in charge of his entire household.

With Joseph in charge, Potiphar's land and household thrived like never before. It was unbelievable. Potiphar stood on the table and looked out across his homestead. He leapt up and down on the table with glee because THE LORD WAS WITH JOSEPH.

Potiphar was full of joy and went around singing, "Things could not be any better." And although it was a popular Israeli tune, he couldn't remember the rest of the lyrics, so he just made them up as he walked offstage.

Joseph was extremely attractive. Every day he would practice posing his muscular body in front of the mirror (the one that faces the audience). His muscles burst out of his clothes. He did several push-ups, the last few with just one arm. He even tried a no-arm push-up. As Joseph was working out, Potiphar's wife walked in on Joseph.

She called to him in a very seductive voice, "Oh, lover-boy."

Joseph, still flexing and working out, said "Hello, Mrs. Potiphar's wife."

She said in an even more seductive voice, "Why don't you stop what you are doing and come to bed with me?"

Joseph stood there in shock. After checking out Potiphar's wife, he jumped up on the table and declared, "I am responsible for this entire household! All of it is at my disposal. The only thing I can't have is you. Away from me, foul temptress!" Potiphar's wife stormed off quite furiously. Joseph left the other way. The next day, Potiphar's wife attempted to get him to sleep with her again and Joseph refused because THE LORD WAS WITH JOSEPH.

A few days later, Joseph arrived at the house to take care of his duties but he noticed that no one was around. Joseph shouted, "Hello!" No one answered, so again he shouted, "Hello!" This time there came an answer.

A sultry, alluring voice answered back, "Hello, my love bug, Joseph." Potiphar's wife seized Joseph by the shirt and said, "Come to bed with me."

Joseph refused. He shook his head violently. She wouldn't let go of his shirt. So, in order to escape, he wiggled his way out of his shirt and ran away, leaving it in her hand.

As she held his shirt, she panicked and shouted to the servants, "That Hebrew slave tried to take advantage of me. Look, I have his shirt in my hand to prove it."

Just then Potiphar walked in and was overcome with anger. He was steaming. He jumped up and down and said, "That loser

Joseph!" Still unable to control his rage, he kicked over the table. He picked up the axe and began to hit the table. At the peak of his rage he shouted, "ENDSAY OSEPHJAY OOTAY AILJAY!" That's pig Latin for "Send Joseph to jail."

Even in jail Joseph proved he was an exceptional leader and God honored him because THE LORD WAS WITH JOSEPH.

END

God speaks to Moses through a burning bush, Exodus 3

Look Who's Talking

Bible text

¹Now Moses was tending the flock of Jethro his father-in-law, the priest of Midian, and he led the flock to the far side of the desert and came to Horeb, the mountain of God. ²There the angel of the Lord appeared to him in flames of fire from within a bush. Moses saw that though the bush was on fire it did not burn up. ³So Moses thought, "I will go over and see this strange sight—why the bush does not burn up."

⁴When the Lord saw that he had gone over to look, God called to him from within the bush, "Moses! Moses!" And Moses said, "Here I am."

⁵"Do not come any closer," God said. "Take off your sandals, for the place where you are standing is holy ground." ⁶Then he said, "I am the God of your father, the God of Abraham, the God of Isaac and the God of Jacob." At this, Moses hid his face, because he was afraid to look at God.

⁷The Lord said, "I have indeed seen the misery of my people in Egypt. I have heard them crying out because of their slave drivers, and I am concerned about their suffering. ⁸So I have come down to rescue them from the hand of the Egyptians and to bring them up out of that land into a good and spacious land, a land flowing with milk and honey—the home of the Canaanites, Hittites, Amorites, Perizzites, Hivites and Jebusites. ⁹And now the cry of the Israelites has reached me, and I have seen the way the Egyptians are oppressing them. ¹⁰So now, go. I am sending you to Pharaoh to bring my people the Israelites out of Egypt."

¹¹But Moses said to God, "Who am I, that I should go to Pharaoh and bring the Israelites out of Egypt?"

¹²And God said, "I will be with you. And this will be the sign to you that it is I who have sent you: When you have brought the people out of Egypt, you will worship God on this mountain."

Cast

* Moses (guy)
* Moses' staff (girl)
* Sheep (the audience)
* Bush

Props

* Branches for the bush (optional)

Tell the audience to respond to the cues given for the sheep, because they are the flock. Moses needs to have his shoes on when the melodrama begins. An offstage microphone would add a lot to the loud booming voice of the burning bush.

As the scene begins...

Moses walks onstage twirling his staff.

One day a shepherd named Moses was out tending his sheep. First he would move his staff to the left and all the sheep would lean that way. Then he would move his staff to the right and all his sheep would lean *that* way. Then he would do his favorite trick—put his staff straight above his head. The sheep would split down the middle, and half would lean to the left and half to the right.

God observed Moses and decided to speak to him from a bush. The bush said to him, "Moses, Moses!" Moses turned to the sheep and said, "I hear a voice!" The sheep in unison all said, "Baaah." And Moses said, "No, really!" The bush said, "Come here, Moses, and take off your shoes." The sheep groaned. The staff plugged its nose. Moses took off his shoes and walked over to the bush.

The bush said, "I've seen the people's misery—and the way you part those sheep." Moses hid his face in embarrassment. The bush said, "I've got plans for you, Moses!" Moses said, "Who am *I* that you should be talking to me?" Then he realized who he was talking to and said, "Who are *you* that I should be talking to you?" The bush said, "I am the God of Abraham, Isaac, and Jacob." Moses looked at the squatty bush and said, "You're kidding."

Suddenly the bush caught fire and, waving its big flaming arms, yelled in a booming voice, "Throw your staff down, Moses." Moses took his staff and threw it on the ground (gently) and the staff began slithering around like a snake, hissing at Moses. Moses cowered in a corner and stuttered to the bush, "Okay, n-n-not k-k-kidding."

As the staff slithered around Moses, the bush said, "Moses! Pick up your staff." Moses gave the bush a puzzled look and then turned to his staff and said, "Hey baby! Uh…want to go out sometime?" The bush said loudly, "Not that kind of pickup, I mean PICK IT UP!" Scared half to death, Moses slowly reached out toward his staff (which was still hissing), and when he touched it, the staff immediately stopped hissing and stood tall and straight.

The bush said, "Now, GO! I'm sending you and your staff to Pharaoh to free my people!" Moses stuttered, "B-but who am I that I should go??" The bush said, "Who am I that I should speak?" Moses said, "Good point." And he took his staff by the hand, waved good-bye to his sheep, and headed off to Egypt.

END

The parting of the Red Sea, Exodus 14

The Sea Splits

Bible text

⁵When the king of Egypt was told that the people had fled, Pharaoh and his officials changed their minds about them and said, "What have we done? We have let the Israelites go and have lost their services!" ⁶So he had his chariot made ready and took his army with him. ⁷He took six hundred of the best chariots, along with all the other chariots of Egypt, with officers over all of them. ⁸The Lord hardened the heart of Pharaoh king of Egypt, so that he pursued the Israelites, who were marching out boldly. ⁹The Egyptians—all Pharaoh's horses and chariots, horsemen and troops—pursued the Israelites and overtook them as they camped by the sea near Pi Hahiroth, opposite Baal Zephon.

¹⁰As Pharaoh approached, the Israelites looked up, and there were the Egyptians, marching after them. They were terrified and cried out to the Lord. ¹¹They said to Moses, "Was it because there were no graves in Egypt that you brought us to the desert to die? What have you done to us by bringing us out of Egypt? ¹²Didn't we say to you in Egypt, 'Leave us alone; let us serve the Egyptians'? It would have been better for us to serve the Egyptians than to die in the desert!"

¹³Moses answered the people, "Do not be afraid. Stand firm and you will see the deliverance the Lord will bring you today. The Egyptians you see today you will never see again. ¹⁴The Lord will fight for you; you need only to be still.

¹⁵Then the Lord said to Moses, "Why are you crying out to me? Tell the Israelites to move on. ¹⁶Raise your staff and stretch out your hand over the sea to divide the water so that the Israelites can go through the sea on dry ground. ¹⁷I will harden the hearts of the Egyptians so that they will go in after them. And I will gain glory through Pharaoh and all his army, through his chariots and his horsemen. ¹⁸The Egyptians will know that I am the Lord when I gain glory through Pharaoh, his chariots and his horsemen."

¹⁹Then the angel of God, who had been traveling in front of Israel's army, withdrew and went behind them. The pillar of cloud also moved from in front and stood behind them, ²⁰coming between the armies of Egypt and Israel. Throughout the night the cloud brought darkness to the one side and light to the other side; so neither went near the other all night long.

²¹Then Moses stretched out his hand over the sea, and all that night the Lord drove the sea back with a strong east wind and turned it into dry land. The waters were divided, ²²and the Israelites went through the sea on dry ground, with a wall of water on their right and on their left.

²³The Egyptians pursued them, and all Pharaoh's horses and chariots and horsemen followed them into the sea. ²⁴During the last watch of the night the Lord looked down from the pillar of fire and cloud at the Egyptian army and threw it into confusion. ²⁵He made the wheels of their chariots come off so that they had difficulty driving. And the Egyptians said, "Let's get away from the Israelites! The Lord is fighting for them against Egypt."

²⁶Then the Lord said to Moses, "Stretch out your hand over the sea so that the waters may flow back over the Egyptians and their chariots and horsemen."

Cast

* Moses
* Moses' staff of wood
* Pharaoh
* Soldiers (one to four)
* Chariot (one for each soldier)
* Israelites (two or more)
* Wall of water (the audience)

Leader hints

Have the soldiers walk behind the chariot wheelbarrow-style.

As the scene begins...

Moses comes onstage. He does not notice the staff on the ground yet.

The Israelite people were sick and tired of being servants to the Egyptians, and they wanted to go back to their own country. When God chose Moses to lead Israel out of Egypt, Moses was very confused. He felt like an inadequate leader, so he decided to work on his skills. First he tried rubbing his stomach and patting his head at the same time. Then he tried doing that while standing on one leg. Finally, he tried doing it with his eyes closed while hopping on one leg. He couldn't do it and fell miserably to the ground. Moses felt like a failure and walked in small circles with his hands in the air, looking to the sky and shouting, "Why me, Lord?" He continued to do this until he tripped and fell over a staff of wood on the ground.

Moses jumped up and kicked the wooden staff. The staff jumped up and said, "Hey! It's not my fault you tripped." Extremely surprised by the talking piece of wood, Moses jumped to his feet. Not ready to argue with the bossy little fellow, he picked up the staff, threw it over his shoulder, and said to the Israelites, "Let's go—we're outta here."

When the Israelites left Egypt, Pharaoh came running onto the scene searching for Moses and the escaped Israelites. Pharaoh squinted his eyes as he looked from the east to the west. While he continued to search for Moses and company, his soldiers arrived riding shiny new chariots. Upon their arrival Pharaoh beat his chest and let out an earth-shattering war cry. He began shouting out orders to his men, "March 1, 2, 3. March 1, 2, 3. April 1, 2, 3." His army marched toward the fleeing Israelites. The Israelites looked back and saw Pharaoh's army rapidly approaching them. They shook with fear and gnashed their teeth. Pharaoh's army shouted nasty things about the Israelites' sense of fashion and personal hygiene. *[Allow army to make up silly names.]*

The ugliest Israelite began to panic and screamed at Moses, "Weren't there enough graves in Egypt?" Moses looked puzzled by the question since he had never counted the graves in Egypt.

The next ugliest Israelite shouted, "We'd rather be slaves to the Egyptians than die today!"

Out of frustration, Moses hit his staff on the ground repeatedly. Attempting to bring order to the chaos, he slapped his staff repeatedly. Once he had the Israelites' full attention, and the staff's, he said to everyone, "Do not be afraid. The Lord will come to our rescue." He was so confident of this message that he repeated it again…this time in pig-Latin: "Uh-thay ordlay illway umcay ootay ouryay escueray."

Moses then did as the Lord instructed. He walked out to the water's edge *[the audience]* and raised his staff above his head. The mighty waters quickly divided into two sides. The Israelites walked through the parted water on dry land. Meanwhile, Pharaoh's soldiers and chariots, still yelling their war cries, chased the escaped Israelites into the parted sea. But in the middle of the sea their new chariots broke down and all the soldiers fell to the ground. The mighty soldiers lay on the sea's floor and cried like little babies. Some even sucked their thumbs.

Moses and all of Israel made it through the dry land of the divided sea. When they had reached the other side, Moses raised his staff above his head and the parted water filled the sea again, covering the crying men of Pharaoh's army. The water karate-chopped, body-slammed, belly-flopped, and kicked the army till they were still and silent on the ground.

Meanwhile the Israelites were laughing and rejoicing at the victory of their retreat from Egypt.

END

Achan Breakin' Hearts

Bible text

[13]"Go, consecrate the people. Tell them, 'Consecrate yourselves in preparation for tomorrow; for this is what the Lord, the God of Israel, says: That which is devoted is among you, O Israel. You cannot stand against your enemies until you remove it.

[14]"In the morning, present yourselves tribe by tribe. The tribe that the Lord takes shall come forward clan by clan; the clan that the Lord takes shall come forward family by family; and the family that the Lord takes shall come forward man by man. [15]He who is caught with the devoted things shall be destroyed by fire, along with all that belongs to him. He has violated the covenant of the Lord and has done a disgraceful thing in Israel!'"

[16]Early the next morning Joshua had Israel come forward by tribes, and Judah was taken. [17]The clans of Judah came forward, and he took the Zerahites. He had the clan of the Zerahites come forward by families, and Zimri was taken. [18]Joshua had his family come forward man by man, and Achan son of Carmi, the son of Zimri, the son of Zerah, of the tribe of Judah, was taken.

[19]Then Joshua said to Achan, "My son, give glory to the Lord, the God of Israel, and give him the praise. Tell me what you have done; do not hide it from me."

[20]Achan replied, "It is true! I have sinned against the Lord, the God of Israel. This is what I have done: [21]When I saw in the plunder a beautiful robe from Babylonia, two hundred shekels of silver and a wedge of gold weighing fifty shekels, I coveted them and took them. They are hidden in the ground inside my tent, with the silver underneath."

[22]So Joshua sent messengers, and they ran to the tent, and there it was, hidden in his tent, with the silver underneath. [23]They took the things from the tent, brought them to Joshua and all the Israelites and spread them out before the Lord.

[24]Then Joshua, together with all Israel, took Achan son of Zerah, the silver, the robe, the gold wedge, his sons and daughters, his cattle, donkeys and sheep, his tent and all that he had, to the Valley of Achor. [25]Joshua said, "Why have you brought this trouble on us? The Lord will bring trouble on you today."

Then all Israel stoned him, and after they had stoned the rest, they burned them. [26]Over Achan they heaped up a large pile of rocks, which remains to this day. Then the Lord turned from his fierce anger. Therefore that place has been called the Valley of Achor ever since.

Cast

* Achan
* Joshua
* The Wandering Jews (a Country Western band):
  Smiley, Hoot, and Earl

* Yahoo (a.k.a. Yahweh)
* Crowd (audience)

Props

* For band members: cowboy hats, sunglasses, bandannas, toy guitar, toy fiddle, harmonica, etc.
* For Achan: a kazoo

As the scene opens...

Band members are huddled on stage discussing the tour schedule.

There once was a good ol' Country Western band known as The Wandering Jews. There were three band members: Smiley, a grinning fool who "played the drums" by slapping his hands on his legs and chest; Hoot, who didn't smile, but he could yodel like a wild man; and Earl, who had no musical talent at all but could hum a great rendition of "Home on the Range" on his fake harmonica, which was his hands cupped over his mouth. Backing them all up was Achan playing his bluegrass kazoo. Achan thrilled audiences everywhere with his amazing combination of line dancing and kazoo-playing skills. Around town the music was known as the original "Kazoot Scootin'" music.

The leader of The Wandering Jews was Joshua, a hat-tipping, YIPPEEE!-screaming, eye-winking country music star. He led The Wandering Jews on successful tours all over Canaan. And let me tell you, Joshua was a ham. He'd face the audience, put one hand on his hip, and shout out a big ol' Israelite "HOWDY!" The girls in the audience would scream and throw kisses. But the guys in the audience got disgusted and hissed and hollered at the clown. That didn't stop Joshua, though. He'd just laugh a big Old Testament laugh and keep on shouting out that good ol' western slang, like "YEEHAW!" "Chattahootchee!," and "Shania!" *(pronounced shun-EYE-yah)*.

The band was on a roll. They'd just played a show in Jericho that brought down the house.

But things were about to take a turn for the worse.

This one show in a backwater town called Ai (pronounced A-I) bombed big time. The band was waving goodbye and throwing kisses, trying to make a dignified exit, when the crowd started to boo and shout out, "We want Garth!" The crowd pointed at Achan and in unison yelled, "Take your kazoo and scoot before you get the boot outta here!" It was a humiliating defeat.

Back home sitting around the fire, The Wandering Jews were discouraged. So much so that even their shoulders sagged. So much so that even their lips sagged. *[You can go on with other creative ideas.]* Smiley stopped smiling and played the drums very slowly on his legs and chest. Hoot could only squeak out a mouse-like yodel. Poor Earl sobbed uncontrollably, while Achan played a sad song on his kazoo. Joshua was so mad he tore off his bandanna, threw his hat in the dirt, and lay face down on the floor kicking and screaming.

Just then the band heard a knock on the door. Who could that be? It was their promoter and manager Yahoo. Surprised to see him there, The Wandering Jews looked at him in awe, and together said adoringly, "It's Yahoo." He shook his head in disgust and said, "No, guys, it's not Yahoo, it's Yahweh." And in his southern accent he told the boys the truth of what was going on. "You guys won't make it to the Promised Land of Nashville because you have broken your contract with me."

Clearing their ears, rubbing their eyes, and scratching their heads with confusion, the boys said, "Who us?," "Shazam!" and "Golly, Yahweh."

Everybody, that is, except for Achan, who just went on blowing into his kazoo and staring at the floor.

Yahweh said to Joshua, "Do you know one of the dudes in your band has been cheatin', stealin', and breakin' promises?" Joshua replied, "No, but hum a few bars. It sounds like a great idea for a song."

But then Joshua got mad. He paced. He steamed. He rolled his eyes. He was ready to charge like a bull. Somebody's greed and self-ishness had fouled up the whole tour for his band.

It was time to find the culprit. Each member of the band came to talk privately to Joshua. First was Smiley, who shuffled over to Joshua covering his face with his hands so Joshua wouldn't think he was smiling; then Hoot, who was so nervous he began to hiccup uncontrollably; and then Earl, whose harmonica breath was so offensive that *Joshua* began to hiccup uncontrollably.

Next was Achan who, stricken with fear, said, "Joshua, it is true. I have sinned against Yahweh." The other members of the band gasped in horror. Coming clean with his sin, Achan explained, "When we played in Jericho, I stole a Babylonian robe, two hundred shekels of silver, and I got a wedgie of....er....uh, I mean a wedge of gold."

Joshua pointed at Achan and said, "You Babylonian robe-loving fool, you've sinned against Yahweh." The other members of the band were very upset and dog-piled Achan. Joshua ordered the others to take him out and stone him.

Not long after Achan's death, Yahweh began to bless the band with success again. The boys were back onstage, just like old times. Smiley was smiling and playing drums not only on *his* legs and chest, but on Hoot's, Earl's, and Joshua's too. Hoot was yodeling like a fine Scotsman again, and Earl was playing "Sweet Home Alabama" on his fake harmonica.

Joshua said, "We can't let anything come between us and Yahweh's promises, boys." They'd learned an important lesson: It's Yahweh or the highway.

END

Die Hard V: Samson's Revenge

Bible text

[23]Now the rulers of the Philistines assembled to offer a great sacrifice to Dagon their god and to celebrate, saying, "Our god has delivered Samson, our enemy, into our hands."

[24]When the people saw him, they praised their god, saying,

"Our god has delivered our enemy
    into our hands,
the one who laid waste our land
    and multiplied our slain."

[25]While they were in high spirits, they shouted, "Bring out Samson to entertain us." So they called Samson out of the prison, and he performed for them.

When they stood him among the pillars, [26]Samson said to the servant who held his hand, "Put me where I can feel the pillars that support the temple, so that I may lean against them." [27]Now the temple was crowded with men and women; all the rulers of the Philistines were there, and on the roof were about three thousand men and women watching Samson perform. [28]Then Samson prayed to the Lord, "O Sovereign Lord, remember me. O God, please strengthen me just once more, and let me with one blow get revenge on the Philistines for my two eyes." [29]Then Samson reached toward the two central pillars on which the temple stood. Bracing himself against them, his right hand on the one and his left hand on the other, [30]Samson said, "Let me die with the Philistines!" Then he pushed with all his might, and down came the temple on the rulers and all the people in it. Thus he killed many more when he died than while he lived.

Cast

* Samson
* Dagon
* Philistine guards (two)
* Philistines (the audience)
* Pillars (two)

Props

* Four or five pennants with the picture of a fish and DAGON written on it; a paper on a yardstick works great

* Sign to hang from Dagon: DAGON THE FISH GOD
* Blindfold for Samson
* Two pillows
* "Phish" bumper stickers for the Philistine
  guards' uniforms; you can get them at a record
  store or just make them
* Three chairs (two for the pillars, one for Dagon)

Leader hints

The pillars are stage right standing on chairs with arms outstretched to form an arch. Each has a pillow pinched between his or her knees. Dagon is stage left, also standing on a chair. Remind Samson to keep his eyes closed throughout, since his eyes have been put out.

As the scene opens...

The Philistines are holding a Dagon rally. Dagon is perched above the crowd with his arms stretched out in a swimming pose and his lips puckered like a large bass.

The crowd waved Dagon flags and bowed before him, saying, "We're not worthy. We're not worthy." They chanted, "He will *fin* you, He will *fin* you." They shouted, "Up with Dagon, down with Orvis," and "Dagon has given us a *porpoise* in life!"

But the crowd hushed as two Philistine soldiers brought in Samson. His head hung down, his shoulders hunched over, his chest heaved with rage, and pain etched on the lines of his face. One of the guards shouted to the crowd, "Dagon has delivered Samson, the enemy, into our hands!" The crowd started booing and mocking Samson, chanting, "Nah nah na-nah nah!" over and over. The guards bugged Samson, messing up his hair, tickling his ribs, and giving him wedgies. Samson tried to break loose, but the guards held him too tightly.

As the laughing crowd looked on, the guards yelled, "Come on, Samson, entertain us!" But Samson, his chest still heaving with rage, shook his head and scowled at Dagon. He was still mad about the guards gouging out his eyes earlier.

But suddenly he changed his mind. He said, "Okay, I'll do this one trick. You'll love it. It'll bring the house down." In his best David Copperfield [big-time magician] voice he said to the guards, "Let me be tied to the pillars, please." Because these guards were not very bright, they tied him to the pillows. Samson yelled, "I meant the pillars, you fish-heads!" They tied him to the pillars but forgot to take away the pillows. So Samson was well padded.

Tethered to the pillars, Samson looked up into the sky and prayed to the one true God. Everyone saw his lips moving, but they didn't know what he was saying. He was asking God one last time for strength.

As the crowd looked on, Samson began to feel his strength being restored. He started pushing again the pillars. His legs began to jiggle and shake, and his arms began to bulge and vibrate. Then his whole body went into convulsions. The pillars teetered back and forth, back and forth. Samson began to groan and to shout kung fu phrases.

The crowd gasped and said, "Ooooooh" and "Aaaaaah" and "Wow, it looks so real." The guards looked at each other and said, "Something fishy's going on here."

Samson yelled, "Lord, let me die with the Philistines!" The pillars swayed wildly, then collapsed, caving in on top of Samson and the Philistine guards—all of which caused a massive dogpile. Dagon came crashing down from his perch, and the perch crumbled and fell to the ground. Needless to say, it was a whale of a mess.

Samson's final life lesson was that the only strength that lasts comes from the power of the living God.

END

The romance of Ruth and Boaz, Ruth 2-3

Love on a Threshing Floor

Bible text

[1]One day Naomi her mother-in-law said to her, "My daughter, should I not try to find a home for you, where you will be well provided for? [2]Is not Boaz, with whose servant girls you have been, a kinsman of ours? Tonight he will be winnowing barley on the threshing floor. [3]Wash and perfume yourself, and put on your best clothes. Then go down to the threshing floor, but don't let him know you are there until he has finished eating and drinking. [4]When he lies down, note the place where he is lying. Then go and uncover his feet and lie down. He will tell you what to do."

[5]"I will do whatever you say," Ruth answered. [6]So she went down to the threshing floor and did everything her mother-in-law told her to do.

[7]When Boaz had finished eating and drinking and was in good spirits, he went over to lie down at the far end of the grain pile. Ruth approached quietly, uncovered his feet and lay down. [8]In the middle of the night something startled the man, and he turned and discovered a woman lying at his feet.

[9]"Who are you?" he asked.

"I am your servant Ruth," she said. "Spread the corner of your garment over me, since you are a kinsman-redeemer."

[10]"The Lord bless you, my daughter," he replied. "This kindness is greater than that which you showed earlier: You have not run after the younger men, whether rich or poor. [11]And now, my daughter, don't be afraid. I will do for you all you ask. All my fellow townsmen know that you are a woman of noble character. [12]Although it is true that I am near of kin, there is a kinsman-redeemer nearer than I. [13]Stay here for the night, and in the morning if he wants to redeem, good; let him redeem. But if he is not willing, as surely as the Lord lives I will do it. Lie here until morning."

[14]So she lay at his feet until morning, but got up before anyone could be recognized; and he said, "Don't let it be known that a woman came to the threshing floor."

[15]He also said, "Bring me the shawl you are wearing and hold it out." When she did so, he poured into it six measures of barley and put it on her. Then he went back to town.

[16]When Ruth came to her mother-in-law, Naomi asked, "How did it go, my daughter?"

Then she told her everything Boaz had done for her [17]and added, "He gave me these six measures of barley, saying, 'Don't go back to your mother-in-law empty-handed.'"

[18]Then Naomi said, "Wait, my daughter, until you find out what happens. For the man will not rest until the matter is settled today."

Cast

- Ruth
- Boaz
- Grain barrels

Props

* Rake
* Blanket
* Crackers
* Whistle
* Glass of water for Ruth
* Perfume
* Dress

As the scene opens...

Ruth is working in the fields, eating crackers and trying to blow her whistle. From time to time she dips the whistle in the glass of water.

It was morning in Israel. Sunlight beamed across the landscape and illuminated the vast field of harvest grains. As Ruth struggled to wet her whistle, Boaz, the owner of the field, arrived. He was a handsome man and always had his rake at his side. The women in the crowd cheered and ooohed. But the men were jealous of Boaz, so they booed loudly.

Boaz noticed sweet Ruth picking grain in his field. He smiled, cleared his throat, and said in a manly voice, "You are welcome to stay in my fields as long as you need." To impress Ruth, he raised his rake above his head—and with a mighty sweep of his arm hurled it into the field.

Ruth said to the mighty Boaz, "Nice toss!" She looked deep into his eyes. She moved closer to him…and closer still. Wanting to be *even* closer, she took one more giant step toward him.

Now close enough, she whispered to the kind man, "Thank you."

Boaz whispered back, "You're welcome." The two paused for several seconds, gazing into each other's eyes. The room was silent. No one moved. A slow and steady cheer began to rise from the audience, and it soon escalated into mass yelling and whistling. Then the crowd fell silent as they watched the love story unfold.

Boaz walked away from Ruth, never taking his eyes off of her. Since he couldn't see what was in front of him, he tripped on his rake and nearly impaled himself on its sharp spikes. In a moment of embarrassment, he stepped on the end of the rake and the handle flew up and hit him in the head. Holding his head in pain and embarrassment, he ran away.

Ruth knew it was time for her to make a move. She put on her most expensive perfume, slipped into her best dress, and paraded around like a runway model. She posed. She turned. She walked. She blew kisses into the air.

Ruth knew Boaz would be sleeping near his grain barrels that night to prevent them from being stolen. So, not wanting to be noticed, she hid herself among the barrels. She watched him make a bed on the grain barrels, pull a blanket over himself, and fall asleep. In the middle of the night Ruth approached him and uncovered his feet from beneath the blanket. There she lay down. The crowd whistled and cheered.

Boaz awoke from his sleep, startled and confused by the crowd noise. He threw off his blanket and felt around blindly for his rake. Once he found it, he waved it around his head in an attempt to scare away any potential grain thieves. What he found, however, was a beautiful woman lying where his feet had been. He immediately put the rake down again and said to her, "Stay here for the night." Ruth grinned and nodded yes. Boaz threw the blanket back over himself and went to sleep. Ruth knew she shouldn't join him on the grain barrels so she slept near his feet on the threshing room floor.

The crowd shouted in unison, "Ooh-lah-lah." *[Repeat: "The crowd shouted IN UNISON..."]*

The next day, Ruth said goodbye to Boaz and left the threshing floor without being noticed by anyone. Boaz wrapped up his blanket and tucked it under his arm. Then he picked up his rake, threw it over his shoulder, and said, "Three things I love: Ruth, my rake, and my grain." Smiling at his own cheesiness, he threw his leg over the rake as if it was a saddle horse and rode out of the barn shouting, "RUTH, RUTH, RUTH!"

END

Xerxes chooses a new queen, Esther 2

The Beauty Pageant

Bible text

¹Later when the anger of King Xerxes had subsided, he remembered Vashti and what she had done and what he had decreed about her. ²Then the king's personal attendants proposed, "Let a search be made for beautiful young virgins for the king. ³Let the king appoint commissioners in every province of his realm to bring all these beautiful girls into the harem at the citadel of Susa. Let them be placed under the care of Hegai, the king's eunuch, who is in charge of the women; and let beauty treatments be given to them. ⁴Then let the girl who pleases the king be queen instead of Vashti." This advice appealed to the king, and he followed it.

⁵Now there was in the citadel of Susa a Jew of the tribe of Benjamin, named Mordecai son of Jair, the son of Shimei, the son of Kish, ⁶who had been carried into exile from Jerusalem by Nebuchadnezzar king of Babylon, among those taken captive with Jehoiachin king of Judah. ⁷Mordecai had a cousin named Hadassah, whom he had brought up because she had neither father nor mother. This girl, who was also known as Esther, was lovely in form and features, and Mordecai had taken her as his own daughter when her father and mother died.

⁸When the king's order and edict had been proclaimed, many girls were brought to the citadel of Susa and put under the care of Hegai. Esther also was taken to the king's palace and entrusted to Hegai, who had charge of the harem. ⁹The girl pleased him and won his favor. Immediately he provided her with her beauty treatments and special food. He assigned to her seven maids selected from the king's palace and moved her and her maids into the best place in the harem.

¹⁰Esther had not revealed her nationality and family background, because Mordecai had forbidden her to do so. ¹¹Every day he walked back and forth near the courtyard of the harem to find out how Esther was and what was happening to her.

¹²Before a girl's turn came to go in to King Xerxes, she had to complete twelve months of beauty treatments prescribed for the women, six months with oil of myrrh and six with perfumes and cosmetics. ¹³And this is how she would go to the king: Anything she wanted was given her to take with her from the harem to the king's palace. ¹⁴In the evening she would go there and in the morning return to another part of the harem to the care of Shaashgaz, the king's eunuch who was in charge of the concubines. She would not return to the king unless he was pleased with her and summoned her by name.

¹⁵When the turn came for Esther (the girl Mordecai had adopted, the daughter of his uncle Abihail) to go to the king, she asked for nothing other than what Hegai, the king's eunuch who was in charge of the harem, suggested. And Esther won the favor of everyone who saw her. ¹⁶She was taken to King Xerxes in the royal residence in the tenth month, the month of Tebeth, in the seventh year of his reign.

¹⁷Now the king was attracted to Esther more than to any of the other women, and she won his favor and approval more than any of the other virgins. So he set a royal crown on her head and made her queen instead of Vashti. ¹⁸And the king gave a great banquet, Esther's banquet, for all his nobles and officials. He proclaimed a holiday throughout the provinces and distributed gifts with royal liberality.

Cast

* Esther (best if played by a guy)
* King Xerxes
* Beauty contestants (girls or guys)
* Judge (the crowd)

Leader hints

Instruct the crowd that when they hear the narrator say, "THE BEAUTIFUL ESTHER," everyone claps. cheers, and whistles.

As the scene begins...

The king is onstage, shading his eyes with his hand, looking far and wide. Occasionally he spots a beautiful woman and his face lights up with admiring interest.

One day mighty King Xerxes began a search over his vast empire to find the most beautiful and talented woman in the kingdom to rule as queen. The king brought several young women to his harem, including THE BEAUTIFUL ESTHER, who was lovely in shape and form.

As part of their preparation, all the ladies were required to undergo 12 months of beauty treatments. They started with aerobics. Next they took rigorous karate classes in which they punched, kicked, and yelled loudly. They massaged each other's faces and rubbed each other's scalps. When their year of beauty treatment was up they went before a preliminary judge, who evaluated them before they went to King Xerxes.

Each lovely lady walked across the runway in her most stunning and swishy-hipped way. Each contestant sang, "Do, re, mi, fa, so, la, ti, do" as a love song to win the king's favor. THE BEAUTIFUL ESTHER was a definite favorite. They all performed spontaneous acts of beauty and talent before the judge for five seconds, and THE BEAUTIFUL ESTHER dominated this part of the contest as well with a powerful performance of "Do re mi fa so la ti do."

After the preliminary judging, it was time for THE BEAUTIFUL

ESTHER to go before the king himself. King Xerxes was a very smooth and put-together man. He walked coolly and confidently—until he saw for the very first time, THE BEAUTIFUL ESTHER. At first glance, the king slapped himself and banged his head against the wall to make sure he wasn't dreaming. He jumped up and down shouting, "Wow, baby!" Trying to regain his composure, he fell to his knees, wiped the drool from his face, and crawled over to his throne so he wouldn't pass out on the floor.

Esther did a never-seen-before interpretive dance for the king. She continued for several minutes because the crowd was cheering uncontrollably. The king, whose mouth hung open because he was absolutely dumfounded by her beauty and grace, joined her onstage. Together they danced a frenzied, weird dance of beauty. They were Fred Astaire and Ginger Rogers. They were Daffy and Daisy Duck. They were Xerxes and—THE BEAUTIFUL ESTHER.

The king found her to be the most beautiful and talented woman he had ever seen. They embraced until the crowd was quiet. The king placed a crown upon her head and declared a national holiday in honor of THE BEAUTIFUL ESTHER.

END

Job and the Terrible, Horrible, No-Good, Very Bad Day

Bible text

⁸Then the Lord said to Satan, "Have you considered my servant Job? There is no one on earth like him; he is blameless and upright, a man who fears God and shuns evil."

⁹"Does Job fear God for nothing?" Satan replied. ¹⁰"Have you not put a hedge around him and his household and everything he has? You have blessed the work of his hands, so that his flocks and herds are spread throughout the land. ¹¹But stretch out your hand and strike everything he has, and he will surely curse you to your face."

¹²The Lord said to Satan, "Very well, then, everything he has is in your hands, but on the man himself do not lay a finger."

Then Satan went out from the presence of the Lord.

¹³One day when Job's sons and daughters were feasting and drinking wine at the oldest brother's house, ¹⁴a messenger came to Job and said, "The oxen were plowing and the donkeys were grazing nearby, ¹⁵and the Sabeans attacked and carried them off. They put the servants to the sword, and I am the only one who has escaped to tell you!"

¹⁶While he was still speaking, another messenger came and said, "The fire of God fell from the sky and burned up the sheep and the servants, and I am the only one who has escaped to tell you!"

¹⁷While he was still speaking, another messenger came and said, "The Chaldeans formed three raiding parties and swept down on your camels and carried them off. They put the servants to the sword, and I am the only one who has escaped to tell you!"

¹⁸While he was still speaking, yet another messenger came and said, "Your sons and daughters were feasting and drinking wine at the oldest brother's house, ¹⁹when suddenly a mighty wind swept in from the desert and struck the four corners of the house. It collapsed on them and they are dead, and I am the only one who has escaped to tell you!"

²⁰At this, Job got up and tore his robe and shaved his head. Then he fell to the ground in worship ²¹and said:

"Naked I came from my mother's womb,
and naked I will depart.
The Lord gave and the Lord has taken away;
may the name of the Lord be praised."

²²In all this, Job did not sin by charging God with wrongdoing.

Cast

✳ Job
✳ Animals (audience)

* Three angels
* Satan
* Servant
* God
* Job's wife
* Job's friends (three guys)
* Sign carrier to cue audience, or use PowerPoint slide (optional)

Props

* Sign/slide reading A TERRIBLE, HORRIBLE, NO-GOOD, VERY BAD DAY
* Three halos for angels
* Horns and dark glasses for Satan
* Yellow fluorescent felt-tip marker for God
* Foil shaped to look like a piece of broken glass for Job's wife
* Three Bibles for Job's friends (optional)

Leader hints

First, divide your audience into four sections by distributing four kinds or colors of candy. Have them practice their animal noise when their group is assigned an animal. Second, cue the audience that whenever they see "A TERRIBLE, HORRIBLE, NO-GOOD, VERY BAD DAY," everyone says the phrase in unison.

It might help—but isn't necessary—to be familiar with the children's story *Alexander and the Terrible, Horrible, No Good, Very Bad Day,* by Judith Viorst (Aladdin Paperbacks, 1987).

As the scene begins...

Job comes onstage stretching, yawning, and humming, looking happy and satisfied.

On the land of Uz lived a man named Job who started his day like any other day. He didn't know it was about to be A TERRIBLE, HORRIBLE, NO-GOOD, VERY BAD DAY. First he smiled and waved to his animals out in the field. His sheep baahed, his cows mooed, his camels spit, and his donkeys let out a big hee-haw. Job prayed on his knees and thanked God for all his blessings.

While Job was praying, angels came out and stood behind him. Satan came out too and stood with the angels, trying to blend in. But of course God spotted him right away *[dabs Satan with yellow marker—repeat "God spotted him" until God picks up on it]* and said, "Well, what do you think of Job?"

Satan knocked Job over and said, "I'd pray too if I had what he had. What if I took it away?"

God said, "He wouldn't stop praying anyway."

Satan said, "Oh yeah? Watch this!" The angels cried, "Poor Job!" and flew offstage. Job got back up on his knees and kept praying.

Just then one of Job's servants came running up, gasping for air, grabbed Job, and said, "Your house is gone, and your children are dead!" Satan let out a sinister laugh. Job tore his clothes, fell to the ground, and kept praying. It was A TERRIBLE, HORRIBLE, NO-GOOD, VERY BAD DAY.

Job's wife came out and grabbed Job by the collar, shaking him as she said, "Why are you praying? Curse God and die!"

Satan said, "I *like* this woman!" Then he put his hand on Job's head, and Job developed itchy boils all over his body. Job was horrified and screamed at the sight of his body. Then he caught sight of his wife and screamed again. Job's wife handed him some broken glass to scratch himself with and walked away. The audience cheered because she was gone. Job stayed on his knees, scratching his boils and praying.

Job's three friends came and surrounded him, repeating in unison "Repent, Job!" Satan came over and high-fived the three friends, saying, "*You* know the man!" Job kept praying and scratching his boils. Finally Job's friends gave up and left. The angels flew in and knocked Satan to the ground. They surrounded Job, comforting him with hugs and kisses on the cheek. Job was filled with joy because some of his prayers were finally answered.

Eventually God healed Job and gave him more children and a new perspective on life. He learned that God is good even when you're having A TERRIBLE, HORRIBLE, NO-GOOD, VERY BAD DAY.

END

Elijah and the prophets of Baal, 1 Kings 18

The Day Baal Bailed

Bible text

22Then Elijah said to them, "I am the only one of the Lord's prophets left, but Baal has four hundred and fifty prophets. 23Get two bulls for us. Let them choose one for themselves, and let them cut it into pieces and put it on the wood but not set fire to it. I will prepare the other bull and put it on the wood but not set fire to it. 24Then you call on the name of your god, and I will call on the name of the Lord. The god who answers by fire—he is God."

Then all the people said, "What you say is good."

25Elijah said to the prophets of Baal, "Choose one of the bulls and prepare it first, since there are so many of you. Call on the name of your god, but do not light the fire." 26So they took the bull given them and prepared it.

Then they called on the name of Baal from morning till noon. "O Baal, answer us!" they shouted. But there was no response; no one answered. And they danced around the altar they had made.

27At noon Elijah began to taunt them. "Shout louder!" he said. "Surely he is a god! Perhaps he is deep in thought, or busy, or traveling. Maybe he is sleeping and must be awakened." 28So they shouted louder and slashed themselves with swords and spears, as was their custom, until their blood flowed. 29Midday passed, and they continued their frantic prophesying until the time for the evening sacrifice. But there was no response, no one answered, no one paid attention.

30Then Elijah said to all the people, "Come here to me." They came to him, and he repaired the altar of the Lord, which was in ruins. 31Elijah took twelve stones, one for each of the tribes descended from Jacob, to whom the word of the Lord had come, saying, "Your name shall be Israel." 32With the stones he built an altar in the name of the Lord, and he dug a trench around it large enough to hold two seahs of seed. 33He arranged the wood, cut the bull into pieces and laid it on the wood. Then he said to them, "Fill four large jars with water and pour it on the offering and on the wood."

34"Do it again," he said, and they did it again.

"Do it a third time," he ordered, and they did it the third time. 35The water ran down around the altar and even filled the trench.

36At the time of the sacrifice, the prophet Elijah stepped forward and prayed: "O Lord, God of Abraham, Isaac, and Israel, let it be known today that you are God in Israel and that I am your servant and have done all these things at your command. 37Answer me, O Lord, answer me, so these people will know that you, O Lord, are God, and that you are turning their hearts back again."

38Then the fire of the Lord fell and burned up the sacrifice, the wood, the stones and the soil, and also licked up the water in the trench.

39When all the people saw this, they fell prostrate and cried, "The Lord—he is God! The Lord—he is God!"

Cast

* Elijah
* Ahab
* Two to six prophets of Baal
* Play-by-play announcer Al
* Color analyst Larry
* Altar
* Bull
* Three or four people to be a wall of fire

Props

* Desk
* Empty barrel for Elijah to pour "water" out of
  (or put in a little water to pour on the poor altar)

As the scene begins...

Sportscasters Al and Larry take their places behind the sports desk, chatting about sports and the evening's broadcast.

Tonight would be different than the usual Monday night grid-iron, but the tense atmosphere of competition was the same. Tonight's event would be a showdown for the ages. In his best on-camera voice Al said to the audience, "A capacity crowd has gathered here tonight—" He paused and flashed his biggest, brightest, most dramatic smile and continued, "—to watch the prophets of Baal and their entire cast and crew take on Elijah, a single prophetic warrior of the living God."

Larry joined in with his most authentic cowboy drawl. "That's right, Al. The hundreds of members of Ahab's team are heavily favored tonight. What makes this an interesting event is that the underdog, Elijah, is the one who issued the challenge." Larry paused to try to give a cheesy smile like Al, but all he could do was drool. He wiped the drool on Al's shirt and continued, "Yes, folks. Elijah is challenging Israel's reigning king, Ahab." He flashed the crowd a toothy grin to redeem himself after the drool thing as Al said, "Let's take a look at the events leading up to today's confrontation."

The pregame tapes confirmed what Larry and Al had said. Elijah approached the king, called him out, and said, "You poor excuse for a king. You trashed this place. Show yourself, you donkey."

Ahab emerged to face Elijah and said, "The puny trouble-maker from the slums has come to challenge me. Ha, ha, ha. I laugh at you." The king busted out some kung-fu moves accompanied by earsplitting "hi-yas" in hopes of intimidating the upstart prophet.

Elijah laughed to himself and said, "Your idol Baal is nothing. It's time for a showdown on Mount Carmel, your god versus mine. Bring it on, tough guy."

Larry, overcome with emotion, slammed his fists repeatedly on the desk. "Wow, can you believe Elijah? How confident! This is unbelievable." He smiled as he continued to slam his fists on the desk.

Al commented on Elijah's pregame performance: "The prophet does have a surprising amount of poise for being so heavily outnumbered. Let's see if he can deliver." He explained the rules of the competition. "The first prophet to get his god to ignite a bull sacrifice on fire will win," he said, and flashed another million-dollar smile.

Larry, now brimming with excitement, let out a loud "YEE-HAAA!" and said, "Then we'll all know who the real God is." After saying this, he slammed his head into the desk and shouted, "This brings back the good ol' days, doesn't it Al?"

Al responded, "It certainly does, champ," and slapped his partner in the back of the head.

The prophets of Baal carried the bull to the altar, and for several hours (which went by like seconds), they summoned their god with wild moaning and shouting. Their shouts and moans grew louder as time went on. They danced uncontrollably around the bull. But nothing happened.

Elijah taunted them, "Shout louder, you idiots." He continued, "Maybe Baal's sleeping, or traveling, or going to the bathroom."

The prophets did shout louder. They also began slashing themselves with swords and spears. Blood was flowing. Larry went nuts in the studio booth and tried to bite a piece out of the sports desk. He was engulfed in the competition.

After several more hours (which went by like seconds), there was nothing. Not a spark. Not even a little puff of smoke. The prophets of Baal—panting, sweaty, and drooping with disappointment—were helpless.

Then Elijah rolled up his sleeves and poured a huge barrel of water over the bull and the altar, completely saturating the wood. Elijah knew this would add to the power of the miracle God was about to perform. (And it would soak the people who were playing the altar in the skit.) Elijah called on God, "Make it known to these people that you are God."

Immediately, a huge wall of fire dried up the water, disintegrated the bull offering and the wood, and scorched the soil around the altar. The crowd gasped at this sight.

Al and Larry looked at each other and leaped on top of the sports desk, pointing at Elijah and shouting repeatedly, "God da man. God da man." Everyone cheered for the one true God of Israel and his underdog prophet, Elijah. Elijah stepped out and bowed and said, "It's all about God."

END

The Greatest Weatherman Ever

Bible text

²³Then he got into the boat and his disciples followed him. ²⁴Without warning, a furious storm came up on the lake, so that the waves swept over the boat. But Jesus was sleeping. ²⁵The disciples went and woke him, saying, "Lord, save us! We're going to drown!"

²⁶He replied, "You of little faith, why are you so afraid?" Then he got up and rebuked the winds and the waves, and it was completely calm.

²⁷The men were amazed and asked, "What kind of man is this? Even the winds and the waves obey him!"

Cast

* Boat—four to six people
* Disciples—three to eight people
* Jesus (guy)
* Fish in the lake (the audience)
* Wind (guy or girl)
* Waves—two to four people

Props

* Cups half filled with water (for the waves)

Leader hints

This melodrama involves everyone. After you have chosen your cast, let the rest of the audience know they are the fish. Position the boat folks sitting down in a circle holding hands with their arms outstretched. The wind and the waves will make their entrance from the audience, while the rest of the players will enter from offstage. The waves should have cups of water in their hands.

As the scene begins...

The boat is already onstage sitting at the edge of the lake. Jesus comes to center stage and begins gesturing and silently teaching the audience.

One day when Jesus was finished teaching the crowd, he saw a boat on the edge of the lake, so he got in it and lay down to rest. The disciples came running on stage shouting, "There he is," and they pushed and shoved their way into the boat. The load was so heavy the boat began to groan as it moved out into the middle of the lake.

Suddenly a storm erupted and tossed and turned the boat on the lake, which caused the fish to go into a major feeding frenzy. They shouted in unison, "Lean to the left, lean to the right. Stand up, sit down, bite bite bite." In desperation, the fish started biting each other on the ears. (Do fish have ears?)

Suddenly, three great waves came up from the audience and crashed into the boat, throwing the disciples down on their knees and covering them with water. Meanwhile Jesus was in such a deep sleep that he began to snore. Just as the disciples were regaining their footing, a strong wind came up and blew them down. The disciples rolled from one side of the boat to the other and the boat creaked and groaned. Jesus went right on snoring.

Finally the disciples screamed in unison, "We're going to drown!" The fish were stoked. They were jumping up and down in the lake humming the *Jaws* theme song. The disciples took one look at the hungry fish and screamed, *"Lord, save us!"*

Jesus woke up, calmly stood up in the boat, and put his hands in the air. Immediately the wind and the waves fell flat. All was calm. The fish flopped on their sides and lay perfectly still. Then Jesus turned to the disciples, who were all frozen in fear, staring at him with wide eyes and dropped jaws. Jesus said, "Why were you so afraid?" The disciples looked at each other and said in unison, "What kind of man is this? Even the wind and the waves obey him!" (They repeated this phrase because they didn't say it in unison the first time.) Jesus said, "You think that's good—you should see what I do with people!" And the disciples decided to follow him to find out.

END

Peter walks on water, Matthew 14

Sink or Swim

Bible text

²²Immediately Jesus made the disciples get into the boat and go on ahead of him to the other side, while he dismissed the crowd. ²³After he had dismissed them, he went up on a mountainside by himself to pray. When evening came, he was there alone, ²⁴but the boat was already a considerable distance from land, buffeted by the waves because the wind was against it.

²⁵During the fourth watch of the night Jesus went out to them, walking on the lake. ²⁶When the disciples saw him walking on the lake, they were terrified. "It's a ghost," they said, and cried out in fear.

²⁷But Jesus immediately said to them: "Take courage! It is I. Don't be afraid."

²⁸"Lord, if it's you," Peter replied, "tell me to come to you on the water."

²⁹"Come," he said.

Then Peter got down out of the boat, walked on the water and came toward Jesus. ³⁰But when he saw the wind, he was afraid and, beginning to sink, cried out, "Lord, save me!"

³¹Immediately Jesus reached out his hand and caught him. "You of little faith," he said, "why did you doubt?"

Cast

* Peter
* Jesus
* Three or more frightened disciples
* Two waves
* Boat (four relatively strong students)
* Wind

As the scene begins...

Jesus and the disciples are standing together. The boat is nearby, sitting in the waves. The waves aren't moving; the water is peaceful.

One night Jesus sent his disciples out in a boat on a lake so he could pray alone. The disciples climbed one by one into the rickety old boat. It creaked loudly as the disciples climbed in. One of the disciples made fun of the boat. A second kicked the boat to test it. Another punched it to make sure it would hold up in case of a shark attack. *[Feel free to add more if you have more than three disciples.]*

When Jesus finished praying, he looked out onto the water and saw his friends far from shore. Immediately he yodeled at the top of his lungs. Jesus loved to yodel. The audience clapped and cheered at his yodeling ability.

Suddenly, a howling wind came up out of the audience and began fiercely blowing the boat and the disciples. It was as if the wind was trying to body-slam the disciples and the rickety helpless boat. The waves picked up a little and started shaking the boat. Getting a little full of themselves, the waves bullied the frightened disciples, calling them names. *[Leave time for name-calling.]* After the bullying, the waves began to slap the already weakened boat. The waves were on a mission to destroy the disciples and crush the rickety boat, which was aptly named the "SS Whiner."

While the waves were pounding the boat, Jesus decided it was time to help his friends. The waves took a break and fell facedown on the ground. Jesus walked across the waves toward the disciples. The disciples spotted Jesus walking on top of the waves and began howling like lost and frightened puppies. Fear and wild hallucinations overcame the disciples, and one of them began dancing hysterically. Everyone shuddered in fear. They shouted in unison (including the boat, the waves, and the wind), "Look, it's a ghost!"

But Jesus was quick to ease their fear. He yodeled a beautiful tune and said, "Don't worry, it's me. Do not be afraid." And he went on yodeling.

Pushing past the still-dancing disciple, Peter shouted out to Jesus, "If it's really you, tell me to walk to you on the water."

Jesus, halting his yodel in the middle of a truly beautiful note, transformed his voice into one that was strikingly like that of Arnold Schwarzenegger. He shouted, "Come to me, Peter. You can do it. Do it now."

Responding to Jesus' call, Peter leaped from the boat onto a wave. He laughed at the waves who had once mocked him so harshly. Peter began tap dancing on the wave and shouted, "I am the water-walking man!"

The waves were a little mad at Peter and began to move around again as Peter walked toward Jesus. Just as Peter took his eyes off Jesus and looked down, he was quickly swallowed up by the waves. Again the waves bullied Peter. Each wave said, "I'm da man," and "Check me out," and "Yeah baby!"

Jesus (still with his Schwarzenegger-esque accent) shouted out, "What happened to you, Peter? Are you some kind of wimp or something?"

Peter reached out for Jesus' hand and kicked the waves a little as they climbed in the boat. Feeling hurt and defeated, the wind and the waves began to whimper like a lost kitten trapped in a tree.

The disciples were in awe of Jesus and said over and over, "He's da man." The infamous dancing disciple never recovered from his wild hallucinations, so he continued his sweet dance moves. He finally passed out from exhaustion and the remaining disciples put their arms around Jesus and said, "Truly, you are the Son of God!"

END

The Day the Rooster Crowed

Bible text

[31]Then Jesus told them, "This very night you will all fall away on account of me, for it is written: "'I will strike the shepherd, and the sheep of the flock will be scattered.' [32]But after I have risen, I will go ahead of you into Galilee." [33]Peter replied, "Even if all fall away on account of you, I never will." [34]"I tell you the truth," Jesus answered, "this very night, before the rooster crows, you will disown me three times." [35]But Peter declared, "Even if I have to die with you, I will never disown you." And all the other disciples said the same.

[69]Now Peter was sitting out in the courtyard, and a servant girl came to him. "You also were with Jesus of Galilee," she said. [70] But he denied it before them all. "I don't know what you're talking about," he said. [71]Then he went out to the gateway, where another girl saw him and said to the people there, "This fellow was with Jesus of Nazareth." [72]He denied it again, with an oath: "I don't know the man!" [73]After a little while, those standing there went up to Peter and said, "Surely you are one of them, for your accent gives you away." [74]Then he began to call down curses on himself and he swore to them, "I don't know the man!" Immediately a rooster crowed. [75]Then Peter remembered the word Jesus had spoken: "Before the rooster crows, you will disown me three times." And he went outside and wept bitterly.

Cast

* Disciples (one or two guys)
* Jesus
* Peter
* Crowds of people (audience)
* Servant girl
* Fire juggler (girl)
* Street musician (guy)
* Offstage rooster voice—someone loud and uninhibited!
* Rain clouds of sadness (two)
* Sign carrier

Props

* Trench coat and dark glasses for Peter
* Plastic bowling pins or similar item for fire juggler

* An instrument for the street musician (a paper or cardboard instrument would be fun here)
* Chairs scattered randomly around the stage
* Sign reading AFTER JESUS' ARREST
* Spray bottles of water for each rain cloud

Leader hints

Alert the audience to listen for cues for "the crowd."

As the scene begins...

The trench coat is slung over a chair with the sunglasses in the pocket. The disciples are standing in a loose arrangement around Jesus, listening.

Jesus was trying to tell the disciples he would soon die, but they kept arguing with him. "That's not true, you won't either die!" said one. "Over my dead body," said Peter. Jesus said, "That's what I keep trying to tell you. You bozos are gonna run like a bunch of scared rabbits."

"Will not," said another disciple.

"Will too," said Jesus.

"Will not," said Peter.

"Will too," said Jesus.

"Will *not!*" said the disciples together.

"Don't make me bring down fire from heaven," said Jesus. "Peter, you're the worst. You'll tell everybody you don't know me three times before the rooster crows tonight. And you'll curse!"

"*Moi?*" said Peter. "Will not." (The crowd groaned.) "Even if your other disciples run, I'll always stand by you."

Jesus answered, "Will so. Listen to me, fella, you are cruising for a bruising."

Peter retorted, "Anyway, what are you talking about, a rooster? We're in the middle of town."

"Peter, you're aiming for a flaming," said Jesus, and that was the end of that conversation.

[Everyone leaves. The sign carrier carries the sign across.] When the crowd saw this, they said, "*Oooh*, it's a sign!" Peter, trying to follow Jesus discreetly, put on a pair of dark glasses. When the crowd saw this, they said, "*Oooh*, it's a Californian!" Next he put on a trench coat and turned up the collar to finish off his disguise, but a servant girl recognized him.

"Hey, you're one of those followers of Jesus," she said. "Hey, everybody, this guy's one of Jesus' disciples! Let's give him a wedgie!" And she started toward him, a big grin on her face. The crowd cackled wickedly.

Peter immediately stood with his back to the nearest wall. "Am not," he said. "What are you talking about? Jesus? Jesus who?" The servant girl stopped and eyed him. He was trembling violently from head to foot, jumping and burping in alarm. She gave him the one-eyebrow-up Spock look, said, "You're a few bricks short of a load," and left him alone.

Peter, shaken from the confrontation, developed a nervous twitch in his left eye as he walked away from the scene. Next he developed a twitch in his elbows. Then a twitch in his leg. But as he got near the gate, it was the eye twitch that got him into trouble. There was a very pretty young woman in the gateway, juggling flaming torches. The crowd cheered wildly at her juggling skill! But when the cheering died down, the pretty fire juggler saw Peter's eye twitch and thought he was flirting. Startled, she dropped all her torches. "Who do you think you're messing with, pal?" she demanded, putting her hands on her hips and jutting out her lower jaw.

"P-p-p-p-p," said Peter. "Muh-muh-muh-muh." She was very beautiful, you see. Then she took a closer look at Peter. His heart sank. *[Repeat this phrase until Peter acts it out.]* "Hey, you're with Jesus, aren't you?" she said. "He was just arrested, you know."

"I know," said Peter, still twitching. "I mean, arrested? I mean, who's Jesus? Who are you talking about?"

"Oh, *you* know who I'm talking about," said the pretty fire juggler, coming closer and glaring into Peter's twitching eye. "You were with him. Maybe you should be arrested too."

"Dashblammit!" shouted Peter. "I don't know anybody named Jesus!" And he turned and ran. This was hard with his twitching leg, but he managed to get away from the pretty fire juggler anyway. All the exercise cured his twitches, but he stood there puffing and trembling and complaining, "Why am I all of a sudden famous?"

Suddenly he heard beautiful music behind him. He turned around to see a street musician playing, "Nobody Knows the Trouble I've Seen." The crowd cheered wildly at the musician's skill!

"I hear you, brother," said the street musician, still playing. Peter's jaw dropped. "You heard me?" he croaked. "I heard you, bro," said the musician. "Say, now that I get a look at you—aren't you one a'them disciples of Jesus?"

Peter's knees began to knock against each other. "No, uh, bro. I don't know who that guy is."

The musician squinted at Peter suspiciously. The crowd began to murmur about Peter and Jesus. "I saw you talkin' to my sister over there," he said. "And even if I didn't, I heard you myself. You got the accent, man."

Peter panicked. He turned to the crowd, flailed his arms wildly, and bellowed, "Stumfatfulpit—*I don't know anybody named Jesus!*" The whole room was dead silent.

Just then a rooster crowed loudly.

Peter gasped. He gasped again. The crowd gasped with him. "Somebody strangle that rooster," he said. "Roosters are a zoning violation." And he sat on a bench, his lower lip drooping, paying no attention as the rain clouds of sadness gathered around him and soaked his trench coat.

END

Jesus heals a blind man at Bethsaida, Mark 8

The Wizard of Eyes

Bible text

[22]They came to Bethsaida, and some people brought a blind man and begged Jesus to touch him. [23]He took the blind man by the hand and led him outside the village. When he had spit on the man's eyes and put his hands on him, Jesus asked, "Do you see anything?"

[24]He looked up and said, "I see people; they look like trees walking around."

[25]Once more Jesus put his hands on the man's eyes. Then his eyes were opened, his sight was restored, and he saw everything clearly.

Cast

* Jesus
* Scarecrow
* Tin Man
* Lion King
* Disciples (three)
* Blind man
* Audience

Props

* Sunglasses or blindfold for blind man

As the scene begins...

Jesus and the disciples are walking along the road.

Jesus and his disciples traveled through the village of Bethsaida. They played marching games to make the trip go more quickly. Jesus had everyone walk in place to get them in step. Then he had them do an about-face. Then he had them do a left face. Then he had them do a right flank *[and add as many—and as confusing—maneuvers as you'd like]*. Then he said, "Forwaaaaard, *march*! Left, left, left right left." Once he had them marching together, Jesus shouted out in cadence rhythm, "I don't know but people say," and the disciples repeated, "I don't know but people say," and Jesus said, "I was born on Christmas Day," and the disciples said, "He was born on Christmas Day."

But as they neared the center of town, they encountered four people traveling together arm in arm. One of them said, "I'm a scarecrow, and I need a brain." The second one said, "I'm a tin man, and tin hasn't been invented yet." The third said, "I'm a lion king, and I need a movie deal with Disney." The fourth man was blind and he simply kept clicking his heels together and saying, "There's no place like Bethsaida, there's no place like Bethsaida."

Immediately the Scarecrow, the Tin Man, and the Lion King all fell at Jesus' feet, begging him to heal their blind friend. They began to chant together, "Lean to the left, lean to the right! Stand up, sit down, give him sight!" They chanted this for almost a full thirty seconds, at which point Jesus said, "Silence!" The audience applauded wildly because the noisy had become quiet.

Just to lighten the scene and put the blind man at ease, Jesus held up three fingers to the blind man and said, "How many fingers do you see?" The disciples and the blind man's traveling companions roared with laughter. The blind man said, "All I know is we're not in Bethsaida anymore," and he knelt before Jesus.

While the blind man's three traveling companions hummed the infamous "Somewhere Over the Rainbow" quietly in the background, Jesus leaned right into the blind man's face. He clapped his hands twice, looked in the direction of heaven, clapped twice again and then touched the blind man's face. And just like that—it was a miracle—Jesus healed the man's bad breath.

But the blind man still couldn't see. So while the traveling companions and the disciples still hummed "Somewhere Over the Rainbow," Jesus held out his hands for complete silence. All eyes focused on him as he worked up a mouthful of saliva. The townspeople thought he was getting ready to whistle a hymn or something.

But instead, Jesus spit in one of his hands. The crowd went wild with approval.

Jesus held up his clean hand to silence the crowd, and with the other hand he touched the blind man's eyes.

The crowd groaned and yelled, "Gross!" but Jesus quieted the crowd and quickly asked the man, "Can you see now?"

The man looked toward Jesus and said, "If I say no, will you put spit in my eyes again?"

But he added, "I see men that look like trees walking around." However, this was just the disciples, the Scarecrow, the Lion King, and the Tin Man pretending to be trees.

Jesus spit on his hand again and touched the blind man's eyes. And this time, just to make sure his hearing was okay, Jesus also spit on his finger and put it in the blind man's ear. He also coughed on the man's kneecap and burped on the man's wrist.

The man opened his eyes. He started yelling, "I can see, I can see, I can see!" The Scarecrow, the Lion King, and the Tin Man began to yell, "Your breath is better, your breath is better, your breath is better!"

They all came together for a group hug and high-fives, and gave thanks to the Lord for his mighty work.

END

Jesus heals and casts out demons, Luke 4

101 Damnations

Bible text

[40]When the sun was setting, the people brought to Jesus all who had various kinds of sickness, and laying his hands on each one, he healed them. [41]Moreover, demons came out of many people, shouting, "You are the Son of God!" But he rebuked them and would not allow them to speak, because they knew he was the Christ.

Cast

* Jesus
* Crowd
* Damnation (demon)-possessed people (two)
* Offstage engine and brake noise for Cruella's GMC Demoniac
* Norma, possessed by the chief damnation, Cruella De Vil
* Steering wheel for Cruella's GMC Demoniac
* Sun

Props

* Sign reading SUN
* Chair for sun to "set" in
* Round labeling stickers from an office supply store—the more vivid the colors, the better. Put about 20 spots on each of the damnation-possessed victims and Cruella De Vil
* A couple of dog biscuits for Cruella

Leader hints

The right Cruella De Vil *makes* this melodrama. Find a young woman in your group who has a flair for the dramatic and isn't afraid to ham it up. Remind her to take the steering wheel with her when she enters for her scene.

In the opening scene, Jesus walks through the crowd, healing people as he goes. Audience members who find Jesus' hand on them should act or speak whatever you read.

In fact, add a few more creative diseases depending on how comfortable the students are with each other. For example, describe premature hair loss—and Jesus goes to a balding leader. Or a hormonal imbalance that causes constant flirting. Just be sensitive to your group—a good laugh is never worth the risk of hurt feelings.

As the scene opens...

Jesus walks among the crowd, laying his hands on people and healing them. The sun stands at the edge of the area by a chair.

Our story began just as the sun set. *[The sun, holding the sign, "sets" in the chair.]* It had been a long day. As Jesus made his way through the crowd, people reached out to him, trying to touch him so they might be healed. Some patted him on the back, while others gave him a hug around the calves as he walked through the group.

Jesus stopped at a person with uncontrollable burping. He reached out, touched her head, and said, "Be healed." Then there was the person who incessantly sneezed. Jesus touched his head and said, "God bless you." He came next to a person who kept throwing up. Jesus patted him on the back, rubbed his stomach, and said, "Be healed. And clean up your mess before you go." Then, he came upon a young lad who thought he was a chimpanzee, jumping around, making ape noises, and laughing like a hyena. Jesus put both hands on his shoulders, looked him in the eye, and said, "For heaven's sake, stop monkeying around." *[This is the time to add any other creative diseases.]*

By this time Jesus had come to the front of the crowd. Two people covered with spots walked toward him. Everybody in the crowd pointed at them because they were so easy to spot. They were easy to hear, too, because they were barking, hissing, growling, and uttering curses such as, "May you dress like Dennis Rodman" and "May you sing like Marilyn Manson." Because of all the spots, some in the crowd thought that these poor people had the dreaded disease leopard-sy.

It was clear to Jesus that these two were possessed by swarms of demons—101 damnations, in fact. So he pointed at them as you would at any angry dog, and in a loud voice commanded them, "*Heel*! Down, boys!" They both dropped to all fours and began whimpering like scared puppies. One of them, in a completely normal voice, said with wonder, "Well, I'll be doggoned."

Just when everyone thought the excitement was over, from the back of the crowd came the roar of loud engines. Zooming to the front of the crowd [*repeat this line if Cruella doesn't pick up on it the first time*], jerking the steering wheel violently left and right, was a woman the locals knew as Norma. But in Norma lived the chief demon, Cruella De Vil, who had spent all night looking for these two lost damnations who were now calm as puppies. She drove right up to Jesus, yanked backward hard on the steering wheel to help the car stop, and stepped out of her brand-new, sparkling, fire engine-red GMC Demoniac. The steering wheel, gasping and exhausted, dropped to the floor of the car. Cruella De Vil growled at the crowd. She hissed. She laughed wickedly. Enraged and baring her teeth, she barked at Jesus, doing her best to intimidate the crowd as well as Jesus.

Jesus rolled his eyes at the crowd. Then he whistled and said in a confident voice, "Here, Spot." Cruella growled and snarled at Jesus, but Jesus said sternly, "Be healed! Damnations, come out of this woman!" Immediately she began to take off her spots. Jesus pointed and said, "Hmm…see spots run!"

As Cruella De Vil, the chief demon, came out of Norma, Cruella cried out, "You are the Son of God!" But Jesus put his hand over her mouth and whispered loudly, "It's not yet time for people to know." Now calm, Norma began to pet and play with the two others, scratching them on the back, tickling them under their neck, and giving them a little snack of devil's food cake [*the dog biscuits*].

The crowd looked on in awe [*repeat if you're not getting an acceptable level of awe*] because they had just seen Jesus throw demons out of people!

END

Martha Steward and CinderMary

Bible text

³⁸As Jesus and his disciples were on their way, he came to a village where a woman named Martha opened her home to him. ³⁹She had a sister called Mary, who sat at the Lord's feet listening to what he said. ⁴⁰But Martha was distracted by all the preparations that had to be made. She came to him and asked, "Lord, don't you care that my sister has left me to do the work by myself? Tell her to help me!"

⁴¹"Martha, Martha," the Lord answered, "you are worried and upset about many things, ⁴²but only one thing is needed. Mary has chosen what is better, and it will not be taken away from her."

Cast

❋ Martha Steward
❋ CinderMary
❋ Wicked stepmother
❋ Prince

Props

❋ Recipe cards (index cards)
❋ Bible
❋ Broom
❋ Apron
❋ Yellow dish gloves
❋ Dishwasher sponge
❋ Toothbrush
❋ Table
❋ Napkins

Leader hints

Before the melodrama begins, place the recipe cards, apron, gloves, sponge, and napkins in the kitchen with Martha. The broom, and the toothbrush, and the Bible should be with Mary, and the table should be onstage.

As the scene opens...

In the kitchen, Martha Steward is flipping through index cards, while CinderMary is reading her Bible intently.

Once upon a time there were two sisters named Martha Steward and CinderMary, who lived with their wicked stepmother in a small village called Bethany. Every day Martha would stand in the kitchen, reading her recipe cards and making meal plans, while CinderMary sat on the floor reading her Bible, taking a break from her chores. The wicked stepmother walked in the room and shouted "CinderMary, get to work! Why can't you be more like your sister?" CinderMary put her Bible on the table and stared off into space while she swept the floor. In the meantime Martha stayed in the kitchen singing "Whistle while you work" while she rearranged her recipe cards.

One day a Prince came to call upon Martha Steward and CinderMary. He knocked on the door, and when the wicked stepmother peered through the window and saw him, she was so excited she ran to the kitchen to hug Martha. She wanted Martha to win the Prince's affection, so they huddled together in the kitchen cooking up a scheme. Mary tried to join the huddle, but they wouldn't let her in. Instead they pushed her away and whispered to each other a plan to keep her away from the Prince. The wicked stepmother said, "Martha, the best way to impress him is with your household skills."

Martha quickly put on her apron and gloves, took the dishwashing sponge in her right hand and declared, "This is a good thing!" The stepmother ordered CinderMary to get in the corner on her hands and knees and scrub the floor with a toothbrush. The wicked stepmother went to the door and opened it, greeting the Prince with her best curtsy. The Prince entered the room, sat down at the table and began reading the Bible. Martha, trying to look as busy as a bee, put down the sponge, took off the gloves, and made swan sculptures from the napkins on the table, all the while repeating, "It's a good thing. It's a good thing!"

Trying not to be too obvious, CinderMary scrubbed her way over to where the Prince was reading out loud from the Bible. Soon she stopped scrubbing and listened to the Prince with wide eyes and an open mouth. Martha was appalled. She stormed up to the Prince and said, "This is *not* a good thing. Look how busy I am making swans for your dinner table and CinderMary is sitting on her duff. Make her help me." The prince just shook his head and said, "Martha, Martha—you need to read Luke 10:41-42."

Martha let out a disgusted snort and stomped off to work on her very popular, but sometimes boring, TV show that airs each morning on CBS.

The Prince got up from his chair and took CinderMary by the hand. He made her his disciple, and they lived happily ever after.

END

The poor man's banquet, Luke 14

The Godly Gourmet

Bible Text

¹⁵When one of those at the table with him heard this, he said to Jesus, "Blessed is the man who will eat at the feast in the kingdom of God."

¹⁶Jesus replied: "A certain man was preparing a great banquet and invited many guests. ¹⁷At the time of the banquet he sent his servant to tell those who had been invited, 'Come, for everything is now ready.'

¹⁸"But they all alike began to make excuses. The first said, 'I have just bought a field, and I must go and see it. Please excuse me.'

¹⁹"Another said, 'I have just bought five yoke of oxen, and I'm on my way to try them out. Please excuse me.'

²⁰"Still another said, 'I just got married, so I can't come.'

²¹"The servant came back and reported this to his master. Then the owner of the house became angry and ordered his servant, 'Go out quickly into the streets and alleys of the town and bring in the poor, the crippled, the blind and the lame.'

²²"'Sir,' the servant said, 'what you ordered has been done, but there is still room.'

²³"Then the master told his servant, 'Go out to the roads and country lanes and make them come in, so that my house will be full. ²⁴I tell you, not one of those men who were invited will get a taste of my banquet.'"

Cast

* Godly Gourmet (guy)
* Camera operator (guy or girl)
* Three audience members (selected randomly during the sketch)
* Studio audience

Props

* Chef's hat
* Wooden spoon
* Cooking pot
* Video camera (for camera person)
* Table
* Three chairs
* Cell phone (for audience member #1)

❀ Pager (for audience member #2)

❀ Watch (for audience member #3)

❀ Cookies or some other food item for everyone
(optional)

Leader hints

Before this melodrama begins, set the table onstage—this will be the kitchen. Tape signs reading YOU'VE WON! COME ON DOWN! to the underside of three chairs in the audience. Put the cell phone near the first chair, the pager near the second chair, and the watch near the third chair. Place some type of food in the bottom of the chef's cooking pot (candy bars or chocolate kisses) for the audience, who will rush the stage at the end of the melodrama.

Cast the Godly Gourmet and the camera person before the drama begins. The three audience members will be cast spontaneously during the sketch. Since the signs are taped to the bottom of chairs, you have limited control over which students are selected. You may have to adapt the narration slightly depending on whether girls or guys come forward (or it might be funny to leave the dialogue the way it is anyway).

When it's time for the three audience members to come onstage, they should pull the chairs up to the table to sit.

As the scene opens...

The camera person is signaling the start of "The Godly Gourmet" show with a large hand motion—a 5-4-3-2-1 countdown.

There once was a very popular TV show called "The Godly Gourmet" hosted by a French chef with an accent so thick you could hardly understand him. Everyone loved the show because "The Godly Gourmet" would dance around the kitchen, move with almost ridiculously big motions, and speak with his funny French accent. Each week the studio audience of the show would burst into applause when the chef of the show rushed into the kitchen. He would put on his chef's hat, pick up his wooden spoon, and quote Bible verses from memory while he stirred that day's special recipe. (If he couldn't think of any texts, he would just make them up.) The smell of his cooking was so delicious, it made the studio audience drool. They drooled a lot. In fact, it was common that they would drool on each other.

Once a year the Godly Gourmet invited people from the studio audience to join him onstage for a special meal. The people who paid the most for their seats had invitations under their chairs and were the lucky winners. These audience members came running up onto the stage waving to the cameras while the rest of the audience applauded. When they walked by the camera person, they wanted him to see how expensive their clothes were, so they flashed their labels, posed in exaggerated supermodel poses, and flirted with the camera.

Once they got onstage and sat down at the table, they started comparing their outfits and sizing each other up.

Then the Godly Gourmet came out with a big dish for them. Suddenly the first audience member's cell phone rang. He couldn't find it right away, so it rang quite a few times till he eventually found it. After talking loudly on the phone as if no one else were in the room, he finally hung up. He stood up and said in a booming and commanding voice, "*I'm* the boss of a large company, and I have to go fire some employees." And he hurried away.

The chef leaped across the kitchen in order to focus again, and once again began serving up the delectable dish, when the second audience member got paged. He pulled out his pager, stood up suddenly, and said in a snooty "I make lots of money" voice, "My Internet stock just went up, and I have to buy more, more, more before the market closes!" And he hurried away too.

Before the chef could start serving again, the third audience member looked at her watch and shouted, "Oh no! I'm getting my nose hairs waxed in 10 minutes!" And she ran off.

The Godly Gourmet looked at his empty table and quoted John 11:35, "Jesus wept." And then he began to cry. First he cried softly—but then he cried big uncontrollable French-accented sobs, with his shoulders shaking up and down so hard it looked like he was at a hard-core techno concert Not knowing what to do, the camera person stopped the taping and went over to comfort the chef. He put his arm around him and whispered an idea in his ear. The Godly Gourmet got a big smile on his face, waved his wooden spoon, and shouted—in his funny French accent, of course—"This meal's for everyone. Come and get it!" The cameras rolled, and the studio audience stormed the stage, running over the camera person, who shouted "Cut! Cut!" Everybody who came to the show that day had the best meal of their lives. Everyone that is, except for three people who were too busy to eat what was prepared for them.

END

Mr. God's Neighborhood

Bible text

[15]People were also bringing babies to Jesus to have him touch them. When the disciples saw this, they rebuked them. [16]But Jesus called the children to him and said, "Let the little children come to me, and do not hinder them, for the kingdom of God belongs to such as these. [17]I tell you the truth, anyone who will not receive the kingdom of God like a little child will never enter it."

Cast

* Mr. God (aka Jesus)
* Disciples (two or more)
* Children (four)
* Parents (one guy and one girl or more if you have enough kids)

Props

* Cardigan sweater for Mr. God
* Pair of slippers
* Tissues for one disciple
* T-shirts for disciples with pinned-on signs: EVENT STAFF
* "Mister Rogers' Neighborhood" theme music if possible (download it from www.pbs.org/rogers/songlist/song1.htm.)

Leader hints

If you can, rehearse Mr. God's theme song with your performer before you perform the skit. The "I am divine" line is a lot funnier if Mr. God sings it without your prompting.

As the scene opens...

Children are seated in a circle, talking with each other and playing Patty Cake, Rock-Paper-Scissors, and the like. If you have it, play the "Mister Rogers' Neighborhood" theme music in the background. Fade out music as the script begins.

It was a jolly afternoon in the Holy Land. The children were playing Holy Landish games together, like Patty Cake...Rock, Papyrus, Scissors...Here We Go Round the Burning Bush...King of the Ark. Everyone was laughing and singing their favorite childhood songs. They sang the Barney song. They sang "Old Man Noah Had an Ark" to the tune of "Old MacDonald Had a Farm." It was a wonderful afternoon.

But just as the kids got to the verse, "...and on that ark he had two doves," two disciples of Mr. God—or Jesus, as he was known then—walked into the circle shouting for everybody to move back and shut up. Those disciples were doing your basic crowd control, warning everybody that Jesus was going to be showing up soon and that all the boys and girls would have to be on their very best behavior. In fact, the disciples themselves started prepping the children—combing hair, straightening posture, helping one little boy blow his nose.

That's when they heard the sound *[play "Mister Rogers' Neighborhood" theme music]* of Mr. God walking along and singing that familiar song, "It's a beautiful day in the neighborhood / A beautiful day for a neighbor / Would you be mine? / I am di-vine...Won't you be my neighbor?"

He gave a big friendly wave and shouted, "Hi, boys and girls!" Then Mr. God began to change into his slippers. He said, "How would you children like to be healed from various illnesses today?" The kids nodded and said all together in their best sing-song kindergarten voices, "Yeeeees, Mr. God!"

Two parents standing nearby picked up one of the little children and set him on Mr. God's lap. The little child then began telling Mr. God all the things he wanted for Christmas. That's when Mr. God told the little child that, sorry, he wasn't Santa Claus, and that Santa Claus was probably an evil influence. The little child began weeping loudly. But Mr. God placed his hand upon the child's head and, in a loud voice, cried, *"Be healed*!" But the child cried even louder. So Mr. God put his hand over the child's mouth and said quietly, "Be hushed." The child's crying did get quieter, but the sniffling and whining he did only annoyed everyone. Then Mr. God turned to the children sitting around him and said, "Boys and girls, can you say 'Rain down fire and brimstone'?" And immediately the child stopped sniffling and whining.

All the little children were so excited about what Jesus had done, they began to sing the Barney song together: "I love you, you love me..." Mr. God put his fingers in his ears and said, "I hate that song!" But did the children stop singing it? No! They just kept on singing. Which is when Jesus threw up. *Then* the children stopped singing, and instead said things like, "Gross!" and "Yucky!" The disciples pointed down at the floor and warned the children, "Okay, kids, don't step in Mr. Vomit."

Then the two parents brought another child to Jesus—a child with a habit of smacking himself in the face. He'd smack his face, then howl like a wolf. Over and over. It was a frightening sight. Some of the little children began shuddering and covering their faces.

That was when the disciples moved forward to block the path of the parents so they couldn't bring the child to Jesus. The disciples got the father in a headlock—a gentle one. The mother dropped to her knees and pleaded with Jesus to heal their son. But the disciples stood their ground and would not get out of the way. One of them even turned and said to the pleading woman, "Either hush or Jesus is going to turn you into a mushroom."

That's when Jesus stood up, stretched out his hand to the disciple, and said, "Oh, knocketh it off." But the disciple *still* refused to let the parents move forward. That's when Jesus turned to the children again and said, "Boys and girls, can you say, 'Rain down fire and brimstone'?" The disciple quickly let go.

And Jesus embraced the little child with the slapping condition (dodging the slaps, of course) and said in a deep commanding voice (between the howls, of course), "*Be healed*!" He added, "And stop crying, wolf." With that, the boy was healed. He got a big grin on his face and began slapping the disciples instead. Just kidding!

Jesus looked out over the crowd and said, "Let the little children come to me. To be a part of Mr. God's neighborhood, you must have the faith of a little child!"

The little children cheered, and their parents shook hands with the disciples and then hugged Jesus.

END

Jesus heals the blind, deaf, and crippled, John 5

The Great Pool Party

Bible text

[1]Some time later, Jesus went up to Jerusalem for a feast of the Jews. [2]Now there is in Jerusalem near the Sheep Gate a pool, which in Aramaic is called Bethesda and which is surrounded by five covered colonnades. [3]Here a great number of disabled people used to lie—the blind, the lame, the paralyzed—and they waited for the moving of the waters. [4]From time to time an angel of the Lord would come down and stir up the waters. The first one into the pool after each such disturbance would be cured of whatever disease he had.* [5]One who was there had been an invalid for thirty-eight years. [6]When Jesus saw him lying there and learned that he had been in this condition for a long time, he asked him, "Do you want to get well?"

[7]"Sir," the invalid replied, "I have no one to help me into the pool when the water is stirred. While I am trying to get in, someone else goes down ahead of me."

[8]Then Jesus said to him, "Get up! Pick up your mat and walk." [9]At once the man was cured; he picked up his mat and walked.

* Some biblical texts do not include the end of verse 3 and verse 4

Cast

* Waves (two to four people)
* Blind woman
* Deaf man
* Crippled beggar
* Jesus

Props

* Walking cane (for blind woman)

Leader hints

This melodrama plays best when the blind woman and deaf man know their staging in advance or are sharp enough to listen for their cues. Feel free to go over it with them before the melodrama begins.

The waves should be lying down on stage. The rest of the cast members will enter from offstage.

There once was a pool that had great healing powers because of the magical waves within it. One day as the waves lay quietly in the pool, a blind woman with a walking stick came up and sat down.

Then came a deaf man who stood next to the blind woman. He was smiling and waving at her. She looked the opposite way from him, put out her hand and said, "How are you?" The deaf man came around to where she was looking, took her hand and said, "Sure, I'd love to dance." He pulled her up and they danced the waltz.

A crippled beggar crawled up to them and said, "Could I cut in?" The deaf man couldn't hear, and the blind woman couldn't see, so they accidentally stepped on the poor crippled beggar and kept dancing. The crippled beggar dragged dejectedly over to the side of the pool, and sat there moping in self-pity.

Finally the blind woman stopped and said, "Let's play marco polo!" The deaf man didn't hear her and said, "Let's play blind man's bluff!" Before anyone could get offended, the waves in the pool started to stir and rise up. The magical waves were healing people. The deaf man saw what was happening, the blind woman heard the commotion, and the crippled beggar said, "Somebody help me!" The couple held hands and, running to jump in the pool, said, "Last one in is a crippled beggar!" When they rose up, the blind woman yelled, "I can see," and the deaf man shouted, "I can hear," and they went offstage jumping and cheering. Frustrated, the crippled beggar sat at the edge of the pool watching the waves settle down.

Just at that moment, Jesus walked in and stood in front of the beggar and said, "Do you want to be healed?" Whining, the beggar said, "I can't get to the pool, I can't get to the pool." Jesus interrupted and said loudly, "Get up!" The beggar stared at him. Jesus thought maybe the beggar didn't understand, so he said it in Hebrew. *[Make up something that sounds funny.]* Surprised to hear the Hebrew tongue, the beggar sprang up like a jack-in-the-box. When this happened, the no-longer-crippled ex-beggar got excited, hugged Jesus and ran to meet some friends to celebrate the Sabbath.

END

Jesus raises Lazarus from the dead, John 11

Dead Man Waking

Bible Text

²³Jesus said to her, "Your brother will rise again."

²⁴ Martha answered, "I know he will rise again in the resurrection at the last day."

²⁵Jesus said to her, "I am the resurrection and the life. He who believes in me will live, even though he dies; ²⁶and whoever lives and believes in me will never die. Do you believe this?"

²⁷"Yes, Lord," she told him, "I believe that you are the Christ, the Son of God, who was to come into the world."

²⁸And after she had said this, she went back and called her sister Mary aside. "The Teacher is here," she said, "and is asking for you." ²⁹When Mary heard this, she got up quickly and went to him. ³⁰Now Jesus had not yet entered the village, but was still at the place where Martha had met him. ³¹When the Jews who had been with Mary in the house, comforting her, noticed how quickly she got up and went out, they followed her, supposing she was going to the tomb to mourn there.

³²When Mary reached the place where Jesus was and saw him, she fell at his feet and said, "Lord, if you had been here, my brother would not have died."

³³When Jesus saw her weeping, and the Jews who had come along with her also weeping, he was deeply moved in spirit and troubled. ³⁴"Where have you laid him?" he asked.

"Come and see, Lord," they replied.

³⁵Jesus wept.

³⁶Then the Jews said, "See how he loved him!"

³⁷But some of them said, "Could not he who opened the eyes of the blind man have kept this man from dying?"

³⁸Jesus, once more deeply moved, came to the tomb. It was a cave with a stone laid across the entrance. ³⁹"Take away the stone," he said.

"But, Lord," said Martha, the sister of the dead man, "by this time there is a bad odor, for he has been there four days."

⁴⁰Then Jesus said, "Did I not tell you that if you believed, you would see the glory of God?"

⁴¹So they took away the stone. Then Jesus looked up and said, "Father, I thank you that you have heard me. ⁴²I knew that you always hear me, but I said this for the benefit of the people standing here, that they may believe that you sent me."

⁴³When he had said this, Jesus called in a loud voice, "Lazarus, come out!" ⁴⁴The dead man came out, his hands and feet wrapped with strips of linen, and a cloth around his face.

Jesus said to them, "Take off the grave clothes and let him go."

Cast

* Jesus
* Lazarus (the brother of Mary and Martha)
* Bystanders (four)
* Mary
* Martha
* Sign carrier

Props

* Nun's habits for Mary and Martha, or black scarves to be tied over and behind the head
* Toilet paper for Lazarus' grave clothes
* Three chairs for Lazarus' bed
* Pillow for Lazarus' bed
* Small cup of water sitting beside Lazarus' bed
* Sign reading FOUR DAYS LATER
* Sign reading DEATH ROW
* Photo album

Leader hints

You may need to go over the groaning cue in the second sentence with Mary, Martha, and Lazarus before starting the melodrama. Lazarus will need to get wrapped fairly quickly between the second and last scenes.

As the scene opens...

Lazarus is lying across two or three chairs, obviously very sick and near death. Sisters Mary and Martha are sitting beside him, worried.

It was a sad day at the convent. Sisters Mary and Martha sat by their brother Lazarus, moaning and groaning in obvious pain—Lazarus was groaning, not the sisters. His high fever made for some restless sleep. At one point he began to hallucinate in his dreams and talk in his sleep. First he imagined he was Mick Jagger and was on stage singing with the Rolling Stones. Next he was Sylvester Stallone in *Rocky*, yelling for Adrian. Then he imagined ants were crawling all over his body. And when he was in deep REM sleep he dreamed he was in a really corny melodrama, and he woke up screaming.

Mary and Martha began to slap him repeatedly around the face and upper body to break him of his hallucinations. But that didn't work, so they grabbed the convenient cup of water sitting nearby and splashed him—okay, *doused* him—with the water. Lazarus awoke violently and in a screechy voice cried, "I'm melting, I'm melting!"

His sisters checked immediately for signs of sickness. They checked for a fever, they hit his knees and poked at his eyes to check his reflexes, they checked his pulse. Then they asked him to open his mouth, stick out his tongue, and say (*in a Wicked Witch of the West voice*), "How 'bout a little fire, scarecrow?" Okay, maybe they didn't.

They had just finished the checkup when Lazarus began to choke, groan, and gasp for air. After doing that for a while, he slumped to his pillow, dead as a doornail.

As a final farewell Lazarus' sisters sang to him their favorite song from "The Sound of Music"— "So long, farewell, it's time to say goodbye; adieu, adieu, too bad you had to die."

[*Sign carrier crosses stage with sign reading* FOUR DAYS LATER.]

Back at the convent, Mary and Martha were weeping uncontrollably and wringing their hands. Finally they calmed themselves and browsed through a photo album, remembering good times spent with their brother Lazarus. Martha said, "I don't get it. It's been four whole days since we e-mailed Jesus to tell him Lazarus died. Where is he?"

Just then, there was a knock at the door. Jesus walked in and kissed the sisters on the hand. He patted them on the head and tried to assure them that four days really wasn't a long time to be dead. He said, "After all, I am the resurrection and the life." Mary and Martha looked at each other and said, "Whatever." Jesus huddled them together for a big group hug. Then the three left the house arm in arm, still sad and crying.

[*Final scene opens with sign carrier crossing stage with sign reading* DEATH ROW.]

Swarms of people [*the four bystanders*] were mourning at Lazarus' gravesite when Jesus, Mary, and Martha walked up. Jesus wanted to lighten the mood, so he said, "It's time to get Lazarus out of that grave—I'm dying to see him." That loosened the crowd up. They started laughing, singing, and giving each other high fives...except for Martha.

Holding her nose, she told Jesus, "My Lord, if he's been dead for four days, he is going to stink big time!"

Jesus said, "Look, Lazarus smelled bad when he was alive. But if you believe, you will see the glory of God."

The crowd began chanting, "We want Lazarus, we want Lazarus," and "Bring him back, bring him back, waaaaay back," and finally, "He will, He will, raise you."

At that, Jesus hushed the crowd, faced the grave, and called in a loud voice, "Lazarus, come out."

At the sound of the Lord's command, Lazarus jumped up in shock and said, "Hey, hold it down. You guys trying to wake the dead?" The crowd was knocked to the ground because of the stench and in unison they shouted, "Whew, boy, do you stink!" With their noses plugged they got up and began hugging Lazarus and taking off his clothes—his grave clothes, that is.

What a joyous day it was! Everyone was hugging each other and slapping high fives. God's glory was seen throughout the land.

END

Jesus washes the feet of his disciples, John 13

Sweet-Smelling Servants

Bible text

[6]He came to Simon Peter, who said to him, "Lord, are you going to wash my feet?"

[7]Jesus replied, "You do not realize now what I am doing, but later you will understand."

[8]"No," said Peter, "you shall never wash my feet."

Jesus answered, "Unless I wash you, you have no part with me."

[9]"Then, Lord," Simon Peter replied, "not just my feet but my hands and my head as well!"

[10]Jesus answered, "A person who has had a bath needs only to wash his feet; his whole body is clean. And you are clean, though not every one of you." [11]For he knew who was going to betray him, and that was why he said not every one was clean.

[12]When he had finished washing their feet, he put on his clothes and returned to his place. "Do you understand what I have done for you?" he asked them. [13]"You call me 'Teacher' and 'Lord,' and rightly so, for that is what I am. [14]Now that I, your Lord and Teacher, have washed your feet, you also should wash one another's feet. [15]I have set you an example that you should do as I have done for you."

Cast

* Jesus (Coach)
* Peter (team captain)
* Microphone
* Podium
* Team (audience)
* Cheerleaders (two)

As the scene begins...

Coach Jesus walks to the podium. The team has won and lost together and has battled through a long, tough season together. There's a real sense of camaraderie and team spirit, showed by the team members slapping each other on the back, shaking hands, giving each other a thumbs-up, etc.

Jesus walked to the podium to address his team at the post-season banquet. He picked up the microphone, placed it on the podium, and adjusted its height. The microphone squawked some feedback reverb at the coach as he fiddled with it. But being the wise coach he was, he knew exactly what to do. He hit the microphone repeatedly and kicked the podium over and over until they could no longer shriek. All they could do was whimper.

As the food was being served the Coach cleared his throat and began speaking. "Boys," he said, "I have something to share with you." Jesus removed his jacket and began rolling up his sleeves. It was time to step away from the white boards, the whistles, and the line-up cards. It was time to get serious. Jesus moved toward the captain, Peter, and began unlacing Peter's shoes.

Peter leaped up in surprise, and said, "Coach, why are you taking off my shoes?" Without waiting for a response he added, "I have corns all over my feet, and they stink—bad." Peter strained to touch his nose to his foot in an effort to confirm their awful stench. He shuddered at the foul odor.

The Coach replied, "I don't expect you to understand right now. But later, this will make sense." As Jesus removed Peter's shoe he nearly fainted as Peter's pungent foot-odor rose angrily into his nostrils. Someone in the audience vomited repeatedly. The Coach coughed subtly and continued without flinching.

Again Peter challenged the Coach in front of the team by saying, "Coach, you're not washing my feet!" The crowd gasped at his rebellion.

Without warning, the microphone began shrieking again. This time the cheerleaders, following their Coach's example, got up and began violently kicking and punching the microphone and podium. Peter and the Coach looked on in amazement at the cheerleaders' strength.

After the noise stopped, the Coach licked Peter's eyes *[wait for a good laugh in response to the licking before proceeding]*...I mean, uh, the Coach *looked* into Peter's eyes and calmly explained, "If I don't wash your feet, then you can look for a new team."

Peter leaned toward his Coach and begged, "Then wash my

hands, my greasy head, and my scapula, too!"

The Coach responded, "Peter, you don't need a whole bath, it's just your nasty feet. And don't any of you think, even for a minute, that I don't know what's going on." The Coach knew that someone was going to falsely accuse him of doing his job illegally. He could smell it from a mile away. Or maybe that was Peter's feet.

So Jesus washed Peter's feet. *[Say your next sentence fast, but don't repeat it; let them try to remember what you said.]* The scrub brush antibacterial lather-rinse-and-repeat kind of washing, y'know?

The Coach called three people from his team to come forward and remove their shoes, so he could wash their feet. The malodorous air circulated throughout the room and forced the audience into mass vomiting.

Jesus took his place behind the podium and adjusted the fussy microphone that, of course, proceeded to wail and moan. Peter, upset that the microphone had acted up, executed a full-layout body-slam onto the microphone and podium. The microphone uttered a barely audible whimper as it toppled to the floor and shorted out.

Not bothered a bit by the loss of the sound system, Jesus continued, "Do you guys understand why I did this? A team's success depends on the willingness of its members to serve each other. Get it?"

The team (including the busted microphone and the shattered podium) answered in unison: "Got it!"

Jesus said, "Good." Jesus liked the sound of this so he said it once again, "Get it?"

The crowd said, "Got it."

Jesus said, "Good."

The crowd said, "Got it."

Jesus said, "Good."

The narrator said, "The End."

The crowd said, "Good."

END

Fitness Lessons at the Lord's Gym

Bible Text

[1]One day Peter and John were going up to the temple at the time of prayer—at three in the afternoon. [2]Now a man crippled from birth was being carried to the temple gate called Beautiful, where he was put every day to beg from those going into the temple courts. [3]When he saw Peter and John about to enter, he asked them for money. [4]Peter looked straight at him, as did John. Then Peter said, "Look at us!" [5]So the man gave them his attention, expecting to get something from them.

[6]Then Peter said, "Silver or gold I do not have, but what I have I give you. In the name of Jesus Christ of Nazareth, walk." [7]Taking him by the right hand, he helped him up, and instantly the man's feet and ankles became strong. [8]He jumped to his feet and began to walk. Then he went with them into the temple courts, walking and jumping, and praising God. [9]When all the people saw him walking and praising God, [10]they recognized him as the same man who used to sit begging at the temple gate called Beautiful, and they were filled with wonder and amazement at what had happened to him.

Cast

* Peter
* John
* Beggar
* Gate Beautiful (two people facing each other, making a human arch with their arms)
* Screaming girls

Props

* Exercise tights to go over Peter and John's clothes...go for it, it's funny!
* Exercise towels to go around Peter and John's necks
* Whistle on a chain for exercise instructor look
* Sign reading EXERCISE CHARITY
* Tin cup for the beggar

The gate called Beautiful is center stage. The crippled beggar is leaning against the gate with his cup in front of him. His sign is within reach, but he doesn't show it to the audience yet.

Peter and John, two rather buff former Olympians, were exercise instructors at the Lord's Gym in downtown Jerusalem. They would walk down the street struttin' their stuff and thumping their chests like Tarzan. One of them would do headstands on demand. They would roll up their sleeves and flex their muscles, then give each other a slap on the back and a thumbs-up. When they smiled at the girls they would scream and faint *[repeat until Peter and John scream and faint]*. These guys were strong.

About three o'clock one afternoon they were headed over to the Lord's Gym to do some deep knee bends for their afternoon workout. As they came to the temple gate called Beautiful just in front of the Lord's Gym, they couldn't help but admire what they saw before them. The gate was the most beautiful structure they had ever seen. In fact, the gate was so beautiful it took a bow to the audience. But as strong Peter and strong John passed under the gate, they began to fan the air and hold their noses, because the gate was also very strong—if you know what I mean.

Just then Peter and John noticed a crippled man begging for money in front of the Lord's Gym. The crippled man held up his sign and called out to them, "Hey big buff dudes, why don't you open your wallets and fork over some cash?" But Peter and John held out their empty hands and said, "Sorry, we spent all our money on health food and our cool exercise clothes."

The beggar responded, "Well, how about you let me sell one of your gold medals? I need some cash too, you know. You guys aren't the only ones who need health food."

Peter and John looked at each other, struck a pose, looked at the man, and in unison said, "We don't have gold or silver medals, but what we do have we'll give you."

They reached down and grabbed the beggar's hands so he could stand up. But the beggar didn't move. In fact, with the dead weight of the beggar, Peter and John lost their balance and fell on top of the man. He hit them with his sign, and said, "What kind of apostles are you guys anyway? Where did you learn to heal?"

Peter and John got back up and said, "In the name of Jesus Christ of Nazareth, walk!"

Instantly, you could see power go into the man's ankles and legs as they began to shake and wiggle. The beggar starting beating his chest and screaming like Tarzan. He even took his beggar's cup and tried to crush it—but he couldn't. Peter and John grabbed him again by the hands and helped him stand to his feet. The gate began to cheer and shout "Beautiful! Beautiful!" The gate called Beautiful was so happy it hugged itself.

The excited beggar jumped up and down and shouted, *"I'm healed! I'm healed!"* He was so excited he started doing different kinds of exercises. First he did some jumping jacks. Then he did some push-ups. Next, he began to run in place. While he was running in place, he was singing, "Praise the Lord, I can walk over and over again." [*If beggar does not repeat entire phrase, he should be corrected to say, "Praise the Lord I can walk over and over again."*]

Filled with joy, Peter and John ran in place beside the beggar. People in the temple began to point to the man and shout, "Wow! Amazing!" because they knew this was the same crippled man who had been begging in front of the gym.

Then all three men struck a pose and gave each other high fives and a big thumbs-up. They knelt together for a deep knee bend and prayed with thanksgiving to God.

They had seen God's power in a mighty way.

END

Resources from Youth Specialties

Youth Ministry Programming

Camps, Retreats, Missions, & Service Ideas (Ideas Library)

Compassionate Kids: Practical Ways to Involve Your Students in Mission and Service

Creative Bible Lessons from the Old Testament

Creative Bible Lessons in 1 & 2 Corinthians

Creative Bible Lessons in John: Encounters with Jesus

Creative Bible Lessons in Romans: Faith on Fire!

Creative Bible Lessons on the Life of Christ

Creative Bible Lessons in Psalms

Creative Junior High Programs from A to Z, Vol. 1 (A-M)

Creative Junior High Programs from A to Z, Vol. 2 (N-Z)

Creative Meetings, Bible Lessons, & Worship Ideas (Ideas Library)

Crowd Breakers & Mixers (Ideas Library)

Downloading the Bible Leader's Guide

Drama, Skits, & Sketches (Ideas Library)

Drama, Skits, & Sketches 2 (Ideas Library)

Dramatic Pauses

Everyday Object Lessons

Games (Ideas Library)

Games 2 (Ideas Library)

Good Sex: A Whole-Person Approach to Teenage Sexuality and God

Great Fundraising Ideas for Youth Groups

More Great Fundraising Ideas for Youth Groups

Great Retreats for Youth Groups

Holiday Ideas (Ideas Library)

Hot Illustrations for Youth Talks

More Hot Illustrations for Youth Talks

Still More Hot Illustrations for Youth Talks

Ideas Library on CD-ROM

Incredible Questionnaires for Youth Ministry

Junior High Game Nights

More Junior High Game Nights

Kickstarters: 101 Ingenious Intros to Just about Any Bible Lesson

Live the Life! Student Evangelism Training Kit

Memory Makers

The Next Level Leader's Guide

Play It! Over 150 Great Games for Youth Groups

Roaring Lambs

So What Am I Gonna Do with My Life? Leader's Guide

Special Events (Ideas Library)

Spontaneous Melodramas

Spontaneous Melodramas 2

Student Leadership Training Manual

Student Underground: An Event Curriculum on the Persecuted Church

Super Sketches for Youth Ministry

Talking the Walk

Videos That Teach

What Would Jesus Do? Youth Leader's Kit

Wild Truth Bible Lessons

Wild Truth Bible Lessons 2

Wild Truth Bible Lessons—Pictures of God

Wild Truth Bible Lessons—Pictures of God 2

Worship Services for Youth Groups

Professional Resources

Administration, Publicity, & Fundraising (Ideas Library)

Dynamic Communicators Workshop for Youth Workers

Equipped to Serve: Volunteer Youth Worker Training Course

Help! I'm a Junior High Youth Worker!

Help! I'm a Small-Group Leader!

Help! I'm a Sunday School Teacher!

Help! I'm a Volunteer Youth Worker!

How to Expand Your Youth Ministry

How to Speak to Youth...and Keep Them Awake at the Same Time

Junior High Ministry (Updated & Expanded)

The Ministry of Nurture: A Youth Worker's Guide to Discipling Teenagers

Postmodern Youth Ministry

Purpose-Driven Youth Ministry

Purpose-Driven Youth Ministry Training Kit

So That's Why I Keep Doing This! 52 Devotional Stories for Youth Workers

Teaching the Bible Creatively

A Youth Ministry Crash Course

Youth Ministry Management Tools

The Youth Worker's Handbook to Family Ministry

Academic Resources

Four Views of Youth Ministry & the Church

Starting Right: Thinking Theologically about Youth Ministry

Discussion Starters

Discussion & Lesson Starters (Ideas Library)

Discussion & Lesson Starters 2 (Ideas Library)

EdgeTV

Get 'Em Talking

Keep 'Em Talking!

Good Sex: A Whole-Person Approach to Teenage Sexuality & God

High School TalkSheets—Updated

More High School TalkSheets—Updated

High School TalkSheets from Psalms and Proverbs—Updated

Junior High-Middle School TalkSheets—Updated

More Junior High-Middle School TalkSheets—Updated

Junior High-Middle School TalkSheets from Psalms and Proverbs—Updated

Real Kids: Short Cuts

Real Kids: The Real Deal—on Friendship, Loneliness, Racism, & Suicide

Real Kids: The Real Deal—on Sexual Choices, Family Matters, & Loss

Real Kids: The Real Deal—on Stressing Out, Addictive Behavior, Great Comebacks, & Violence

Real Kids: Word on the Street

Unfinished Sentences: 450 Tantalizing Statement-Starters to Get Teenagers Talking & Thinking

What If...? 450 Thought-Provoking Questions to Get Teenagers Talking, Laughing, and Thinking

Would You Rather...? 465 Provocative Questions to Get Teenagers Talking

Have You Ever...? 450 Intriguing Questions Guaranteed to Get Teenagers Talking

Art Source Clip Art

Stark Raving Clip Art (print)

Youth Group Activities (print)

Clip Art Library Version 2.0 (CD-ROM)

Digital Resources

Clip Art Library Version 2.0 (CD-ROM)

Ideas Library on CD-ROM

Youth Ministry Management Tools (CD-ROM)

Videos & Video Curricula

Dynamic Communicators Workshop for Youth Workers

EdgeTV

Equipped to Serve: Volunteer Youth Worker Training Course

Good Sex: A Whole-Person Approach to Teenage Sexuality & God

The Heart of Youth Ministry: A Morning with Mike Yaconelli

Live the Life! Student Evangelism Training Kit

Purpose-Driven Youth Ministry Training Kit

Real Kids: Short Cuts

Real Kids: The Real Deal—on Friendship, Loneliness, Racism, & Suicide

Real Kids: The Real Deal—on Sexual Choices, Family Matters, & Loss

Real Kids: The Real Deal—on Stressing Out, Addictive Behavior, Great Comebacks, & Violence

Real Kids: Word on the Street

Student Underground: An Event Curriculum on the Persecuted Church

Understanding Your Teenager Video Curriculum

Youth Ministry Outside the Lines: The Dangerous Wonder of Working with Teenagers

Student Resources

Downloading the Bible: A Rough Guide to the New Testament

Downloading the Bible: A Rough Guide to the Old Testament

Grow For It Journal

Grow For It Journal through the Scriptures

So What Am I Gonna Do with My Life? Journaling Workbook for Students

Spiritual Challenge Journal: The Next Level

Teen Devotional Bible

What (Almost) Nobody Will Tell You about Sex

What Would Jesus Do? Spiritual Challenge Journal

Wild Truth Journal for Junior Highers

Wild Truth Journal—Pictures of God